# LIVE YOUR DREAMS

# LIVE YOUR DREAMS

# LES BROWN

AVON BOOKS NEW YORK

AVON BOOKS
A division of
The Hearst Corporation
1350 Avenue of the Americas
New York, New York  10019

The William Morrow edition contains the following Library of Congress Cataloging in Publication Data:
  Live your dreams/Les Brown.
    p. cm.
1. Success.  2. Happiness.  I. Title.
BJ1611.2.B745      1992      92-9039
158'.1–dc20        CIP

First Avon Books Trade Printing: July 1994

OPM 10 9 8 7 6 5 4 3 2 1

*Abraham Lincoln said, "All that I am and all I ever hope to be I owe to my mother." I dedicate this book to my mother, Mrs. Mamie Brown, whose love and guidance have made me all that I am and all that I ever hope to be. Because of her, I learned to dream and to live my dreams.*

*I would like to dedicate this book also to foster and adopted children everywhere, and to those who dare to dream.*

—LES BROWN

# Acknowledgments

I would like to thank my lifelong friend Alexander "Bou" Whyms for being my "memory" during the writing of this book. I am also indebted to my trusted friend, adviser and marketing wizard Mike Williams for his counsel and direction for this book. My general manager, Rhea Steele, contributed greatly with her time and energy to this project. I am grateful always to my valued mentor, Mr. LeRoy Washington, to my brother, Wesley, and my sister, Margaret, to my foster brothers and sisters, Angelo, Leonard, Sharon and Linda, and to my children, Calvin, Patrick, Ayanna, Sumaya, Serena and John Leslie for their love and support and suggestions for this book. My good friends Cheryl Jackson and Jean Carne also offered their assistance and support as did my entire staff at Les Brown Unlimited. My appreciation also to Dr. Talmadge McKinney, Dr. Mildred Singleton and Dr. Johnnie Colemon for believing in me. In addition, Thea Flaum and Jack Wilson helped me conceive of this project and contributed in bringing it to reality, as did my literary agent, Raphael Sagalyn, and my attorney, Katherine Lauderdale. Special thanks to Wes Smith, for taking my message from the spoken word to the printed page, and my thanks also to his wife, Sarah, and their children, Andrew and Jessica, for their hospitality and encouragement. And finially, my thanks go to my editor, Paul Bresnick, and his assistant, Mark Garofalo, for their invaluable assistance.

# Contents

# CONTENTS

# LIVE YOUR DREAMS

# One

# Mrs. Mamie Brown's Baby Boy

*When I was young, I danced up this world.*
*—MRS. MAMIE BROWN*

We called the few blocks that were my territory as a boy "The Alley" and they had an alley's nature. It could get tough, so we had to be tough.

My adoptive mother, Mrs. Mamie Brown, tells the story about the time I was coming home from the grocery store with a big bag of rice and a can of kerosene and she heard the new neighbor yell to two of his own sons, "Jump on that boy and beat him up!"

I think the neighbor had tired of watching his boys wrestle with each other so he decided they'd do better to tussle with me.

When Mama heard the neighbor sic his boys on me, she rushed to the door. She saw that they were all over me and that I was not fighting back. You see, my mother had done a very thorough job of instilling in me the importance of preserving groceries *at all costs* when I went to the store for her.

Mama had no husband and very little money. She had adopted my twin brother and me as infants. She worked hard as a cafeteria cook, maid and fruit picker to keep us in groceries. She could not and did not tolerate wastefulness.

I was not always an obedient son but through the effective use of a tree switch, Mama had taught me this particular lesson *very* well. And so, even though I was taking an awful whupping from those two boys, I held on to my Mama's groceries and tried to get a kick in now and then.

But when my Mama came out and saw those boys all over me, she suspended the grocery-preservation rule. "Throw them groceries down and get those boys!" she yelled.

And I did. They stuck to wrestling with each other after that. They learned their lesson. I learned a lesson that day, too, one that I hope to impart to you in this book. *There comes a time when you have to drop your burdens in order to fight for yourself and your dreams.*

Many of us carry baggage from the past that hinders our ability to fight for the things we want in life, our goals, our dreams. If you learn in this book to let go of those burdensome emotions and memories, then one of my chief objectives will be realized; you will be able to pursue and live your dreams.


## My Journey

Let me tell you about my life, and some of the burdens that I had to learn to drop in order to go after my own goals and dreams.

I never knew my natural parents. In fact, I still don't know their names or where they live, but not long ago, I learned just a few pieces of information about them. It was not much, but it was enough. It is still more than I had ever really desired to hear.

Mrs. Mamie Brown, the only parent I have ever known, is all the parent I will ever need. She adopted me and my fraternal twin brother, Wesley, when we were only a few weeks old and on her own she raised us and a sister, Margaret, whom she adopted five years later.

The facts that I recently discovered concerning my natural parents are these: My birth mother came to Miami from somewhere else to give birth to my brother and me on the floor of an abandoned building and to then give us away three weeks later.

This woman was married to a soldier stationed overseas but had become pregnant by another man. She wanted to have us and give us away before her husband found out about us. Those are the facts related to me by a friend of my adoptive mother. I have never discussed the matter with Mama.

For a long, long time, I hated my natural parents, even though I have no idea who they were. It was a lot of work holding that grudge. I didn't even have a picture to glare at. Finally, I dropped that baggage though, after contemplating a quote from the philospher Kahlil Gibran, who said that our parents bring us into the world, but in the end, we are responsible for what we become. Parents, he said, are like the archer's bow and their children the arrows.

*"Our children come through us, but not from us,"* Gibran wrote.

My anger was eased too by a friend's reminder that as an adopted child, I was *chosen by love, rather than being delivered by fate* to my Mama, Mrs. Mamie Brown.

As a child and into adulthood, I had occasionally gone through the same inner questions that come to most who are adopted. I wondered what my father and mother looked like, what kind of people they were, if they thought about me.

I never attempted to identify or locate my natural parents but one time a friend of mine who was adopted did, and he took me along for support. I watched from the curb when his father opened the door. Immediately I saw that the likeness was stunning. This was obviously his true father.

My friend said, "Hi, I'm your son."

And his father said, "I don't have a son," and slammed the door in his face.

My friend walked away, shattered.

"I wish I had never found him," he said. "At least I would not have to live with the rejection that even now he doesn't want me."

Not all searches for birth parents end that way, of course, but I've come to feel that whoever my parents are, I forgive them. I have to play with the hand dealt me and I cannot be effective in my life if I allow myself to be burdened with anger, resentment, regret and guilt.

## The Past Is Past

You can make decisions like that about your life. If you are carrying strong feelings about something that happened in your past, they may hinder your ability to live in the present. You have to get rid of them. They have no real value in themselves, only the value that you give them.

My goal in this book is to help you make this a great life, to help you expand your consciousness—the focused force of your will—so that you may grow and flourish in pursuit of your dreams as I have.

A focused consciousness will enable you to drop the burdens that you have carried and to overcome life's inevitable blows. It can put you in control of your own life. It can also help you contribute to the lives of those you encounter and the world we all inhabit.

You may not accomplish every goal you set—no one does—but what really matters is having goals and going after them wholeheartedly. In the end, *it is the person you become, not the things you achieve, that is most important.*

I learned from my mother that there is greatness in all of us, and that all of us are delivered to this world with a mission. I believe that life is a journey, often difficult and sometimes incredibly cruel, but we are well equipped for it if only we tap into our talents and gifts and allow them to blossom.

I feel blessed to have been the son of Mamie Brown, my role model in life. My Mama is a woman of tremendous determination and courage. Now in her eighties, she is as much as ever a force to be reckoned with. Truly, she is the mistress of her own destiny, a woman who lives her dreams through sheer force of will.

I will refer to her frequently in this book because I am very much my adopted mother's son. The source of my own determination is her great strength. I have learned from my mother and my goal is to impart some of her strength and wisdom to you, along with some methods of endurance and perseverance that I have acquired through my own experiences.

## She Danced Up This World

Mama often told me stories from her own life. She spent her own childhood without benefit of a mother. It is believed that her mother was poisoned by a woman who wanted Mama's father for herself. "My Mama died and left me a crawling baby," she says.

That family legend is responsible for one of my mother's lifelong quirks, which she passed on to me through relentless repetition. "Never put down a drinking glass, leave it and then return and drink from it." She believes that was how her mother was killed—that poison was poured into her drinking glass left on a table.

Her father was a farm worker who followed the fruit crops as they ripened in the southern states. Mama accompanied his migrations and had a succession of baby-sitters, some kinfolks, some not. Though she yearned for a mother's love and the nurturing warmth of a family, Mama's life was not without love or joy. "People liked me," she tells me. "When I was young, I danced up this world."

I have spent many hours in the thrall of stories from my mother's girlhood in rural Florida, tales of her pony rescuing Mama by finding her father and bringing him to her when she was stuck in a tree, and tales of the crocodile that she fed chickens to until it grew into a monster that answered her when she called it.

I still get chills when my mother tells the story of the worst beating she ever received and how the spirit of her mother came to her aid afterward.

*My father told me never to go swimming in the pond where the crocodile lived, but I went anyway. I was ten years old and just like my boy Leslie, hardheaded. I rode my pony down there and took my clothes off and went swimming and when I got out, I looked up and saw my Papa coming.*

*I went to running, but Papa followed me to the house and beat me so bad with a buggy whip. Everywhere you could see on my body there was a lick. He beat me so badly that they had to grease my body afterwards with hog lard because we didn't have enough Vaseline to cover all the welts. I was so sore and crying when I went to bed. He begged me not to cry like that.*

*I was still crying there when it seemed that the door opened a bit, but when I looked again, I saw it hadn't. There was a bar on it so it couldn't.*

*Then, all of a sudden, there was a woman, a tall woman, standing looking at me beside my bed. She had a basket of fruit, bananas and such, and she had a great big dog with her. She looked at me up and down and shook her head kind of sad.*

*The dog stood at the edge of my bed and stared into*

*my eyes. His eyes were like lights and kind of paralyzed
me. I felt I couldn't move as long as the dog stared at
me. The woman left my room and went into my father's
bedroom and I heard him making strange grunting noises
like something was bothering him. I wondered what was
happening.*

*After a while, the woman came back into my room
and looked at me. She looked at me again, shook her head,
and then she and the dog left me. I heard a door shut.*

*When the dog took his eyes off me I jumped up. And
then Papa was in my room. "Did you see that?" he asked
me. I said yes, it was a tall woman with a basket of bananas
and a dog. He said, "That was your Mama."*

*He cried and said that he would never hit me again.
I cried too. He said, "Don't cry. If you'll just eat"—I
hadn't eaten I hurt so, I looked like a snake wriggling in
that bed—"and get better, I'll never do that again."*

*He said, "Your Mama told me if I ever beat you like
that again, she'll come back and get her little girl and take
her away."*

*I said, "You told me my Mama was dead."*

*My Papa said, "Yes, but the spirit lives, and if a
spirit wants her children, she will come for them."*

My mother believes that her own Mama did appear that
day. She carries many such beliefs, a lot of old-time beliefs,
such as the one about no cussing or talking when it thunders.
God is angry, she says, and you don't want to risk angering
him further. "You hear God talking, you fools?" she'll say.
"You better shut up now!"

My Mama also swears to this day that she once saw a
live mermaid, actually a mer*man*. She was about eleven years
old and had gone to get some mullet at the Lighthouse Fish
Market. Two men were arguing outside the fish market. One
blamed the other for the hard rain that had soaked the
ground for two days. He said nature was punishing him for

capturing the merman. Mama watched as the other pulled the merman from a barrel of water. It was nearly as big as Mama. With short, muscular, human arms, a powerful chest and a split tail covered with scales. He had mosslike hair, fish eyes and small fish teeth that grinned at her. He was very UGLY, according to Mama's recollection.

Her vivid description never varies and her conviction of its authenticity never wavers even today. I begged that story out of her hundreds of times as a child, and my children and grandchildren have done the same.

## My Mama's Dream

Mama enjoyed a life rich in most ways. It was impoverished only in the monetary sense. She knew that she was greatly loved by her father and she had a full understanding of how hard he labored to support her.

She married at fifteen but left the man after a few months when she learned that, contrary to his promises, he had no intention of allowing her ailing father to come live with them. "He told me a big lie and after that I could not stand him anymore," she says.

Though she was soured on men in general and marriage in particular, Mama still wanted a family. Her desire was as powerful as her will. Always, Mama yearned for the closeness of a family. As a teenager, she was greatly hurt when a friend chastised her for calling the friend's mother "Mama."

In adulthood, Mama often told friends that she yearned for children of her own because, she said, "I want somebody with me in the world besides myself." It was one of those friends who told Mama about a woman who had come to Miami to find someone to adopt her unborn twins. Mama volunteered immediately.

There was another woman in the running but she

wanted only one of the twins. Mama did not believe in splitting up families. She said she would take us both, and the adoption was arranged.

My natural mother made Mama swear never to reveal her identity or her whereabouts to my brother and me. Mama has honored her vow, though I am quite certain there were occasions when she was tempted to send us back. Particularly me.

I was the burden that Mama bore for many years. "Wesley was always a good boy. You were hardheaded," she says. She never lets me forget that.

We grew up in Overtown and Liberty City, the poorest neighborhoods of Miami. They were not slums or ghettos then, but they are often called that today. Few bother to grasp the social and political forces that drained them of the vitality they had when I was a boy. Both neighborhoods were vibrant with theaters and dance halls and churches, all of which rocked with equal abandon at their designated hours.

Our mother supported us as a cook at the M & M Cafeteria and later as a nursing-home cook, maid and housekeeper. She enlisted friends with their own small children to mind us while she worked for wages.

When she took us in, Mama had absolutely no idea of how she was going to support us. She knew she wanted a family, so she made us that and then proceeded to do whatever it took to keep us in shirts and dungarees and food.

Many times people back away from things they want to do, from the dreams they have nurtured, because they cannot envision a clear way to bring those goals to reality. Mama lived by the saying "You must walk by faith and not by sight." She believed that if you summon the courage to go after your dream, life will provide the answers.

## A No-Matter-What Person

My mother had no plan of action, but she knew within herself that she could do it. She was willing to take a risk so that she could grow in her life. My mother is one of those "no-matter-what" people. We may not have gotten a lot of toys at Christmastime, but we always had plenty of food and clean, ironed clothing hand-me-downs from the children of the families Mama worked for.

My mother was a provider, and a protector. She was a *ferocious* protector. I remember when I began taking swimming lessons at the neighborhood pool, I broke out in a bad skin rash. The doctor said that I was allergic to the chemicals in the water.

My mother wanted me to learn to swim anyway, so she told me to go to the lessons and just watch. Well, the swimming instructor did not go along the program. He thought I was just being stubborn and scared and he made me get in the water and I broke out again. When Mama saw that, she had a fit. "You tell that man if he makes you go in the water again, I'll come down there and shove HIM in," she said. The man got with the program.

My Mama's protective instincts were called upon frequently in my childhood, and their reach was not limited to mere physical guardianship. Mama also considered herself the protector of our characters.

She was from humble circumstances but she had strong ideas about proper behavior that she worked diligently, although not always successfully, to impart to her adopted family.

Shortly after I began going to school, I came home one day and announced to my mother that my teacher said that I didn't have to say "Yes, ma'am" and "No, ma'am" to anybody anymore. The teacher was concerned because I referred to *everyone* in that manner, including my classmates. I took the teacher's directive to mean that I was not to address anybody, adults included, in this manner and that was in raging conflict with my mother's strict code of youngster etiquette. She was very adamant about our duty to honor our elders.

When I came home from school to tell Mama of the teacher's orders, Mama was doing laundry in the tub. She was wet from her head to her toes and in a short-tempered state. She responded to my report by slapping a sopping wet shirt to the floor and firing off a burst of profanity from her extensive arsenal.

"You go back and tell that damn teacher that she runs her school and I run my damn house" came the command.

Like a good soldier, I carried out my orders and delivered my Mama's message to my teacher. *Word for word*. And my teacher responded in kind.

Dutifully, I carried her response back to Mama. Again, *to the word*. "Teacher says don't worry, she'll run her damn school and you can run your damn house."

Mama said, "I thought you'd know enough to cut out the 'damn' when you talk to the teacher."

## A Powerful Voice

Early in my childhood, my mother was incapacitated for several months after she dropped a big pot of hot food on her legs at work. We struggled to get by with help from friends and strangers during that period, and Mama looked out for us as best she could.

Around Christmas, a minister from the church around the corner came to our house with some food. His name was Reverend Ed Graham. He came to the door, tall and proper and deep-voiced, and said, "I heard there is a family here in need of food."

I answered, "Yes, sir." He entered with the food basket and I was deeply impressed. I had seen him before on the occasions when I had gone into his church, lured by the power of a voice that penetrated the church walls to the streets outside. He was a master orator and I was drawn to him as a boy to his destiny.

I wanted to be Reverend Graham at that point in my life, but there was a problem with that. You see, most people in the neighborhood considered me to be more a disciple of the minister's competition than of the minister himself.

I was something of a troublesome child. Or, as my mother said recently, "Leslie was always goodhearted but he had a record of doing devilish things. And I had a devil of a time raising him. I'd tell him to do things and he wouldn't do them so I would have to hit his legs with a tree switch."

At first, it was typical boyhood misadventure that got me into trouble. After watching a Tarzan movie, I told Mama I was going to play Tarzan. She assumed I was going to climb trees or swing on a rope. She found me awhile later when she followed a trail of water running from the bathtub. I had poured water out so that I could lie on the floor and swim like Tarzan. Mama found me flopping in a puddle on the linoleum like a mullet in the bottom of a boat.

When I reached school age, I was frequently dispatched to the principal's office for being boisterous. I was addicted to the laughter and attention of my classmates and likely to do anything to get it. I was prone also to playing hooky so that I could go swimming in the rock pit, another forbidden act.

On top of this, I was a poor student. I had a quick and brilliantly profane tongue, but written material was nearly beyond my grasp. I had trouble reading because of poor concentration. Because of my rather hyperactive nature and my poor performance in class, I was classified as "educable mentally retarded" in the fifth grade.

It was a stigma that weighed heavily on my spirit. But it was also a seductive hiding place. If I was not expected to perform as well as my classmates, there was no inducement to try. My lower consciousness bought into the label that had been placed upon me. I believed that I was mentally retarded and I brought in the Fs to prove it. I flunked twice. They said I was slow so I held to that pace.

I floundered for the rest of my grade-school years, always on the edge of being thrown out. But in high school, I came into contact with the empowering influence of Mr. LeRoy Washington.

## My Life's Teacher

Mr. Washington was a figure of note not only at Booker T. Washington High School, but throughout the state of Florida. With a dancer's powerful physique and a lean, expressive face, he carried himself with great dignity, like a king among his people. And he spoke the King's English. Every syllable enunciated by tongue and teeth, projected to the back rows, the upper gallery and beyond to the Everglades.

Mr. Washington was the school's speech and drama teacher and he prided himself upon finding and developing character and talent in his students. He was a dominant force in statewide high-school speech and drama competitions and active in community theater as an actor and director. At one point, he had his own television show that was popular in the Miami area.

I was drawn to Mr. Washington for the same reason I had been drawn to our neighborhood minister. I had always fancied myself an orator of some sort, even though I may not have known exactly what an orator was. In part, I think I was formed by the hours I spent listening to Mama's tales. She is a wonderful storyteller and she passed the tradition on to me.

From the moment I first saw Mr. Washington and heard him speak, I wanted to be one of his star pupils. His students were the cream of the crop. I was not the cream of the crop, of course, but my attraction to Mr. Washington sparked something in me that had been stunted by the label of mental retardation. I began to feel a purpose churning in my mind and soul.

I became his shadow. Mr. Washington, however, wanted absolutely nothing to do with troublesome me. He scarcely had time for all the good students under his charge. He taught at least five classes at Booker T., and he was always involved in outside theatrical productions.

I could not get into Mr. Washington's class, but my friend MacArthur Stevens was one of his top students. I began hanging very close with Mac, particularly when he was going to do something involving Mr. Washington.

I succeeded in making myself known to Mr. Washington by wheedling my way into one of his plays through a series of white lies and strategic manipulations. The results of my stage premiere were somewhat disastrous, but shortly after that, Mr. Washington welcomed me into his royal court—perhaps more as jester than prince—and changed the course of my life by opening my mind to possibilities that I had previously not dared to dream of. I will relate those stories later.

## The Gift of Self-esteem

Mr. Washington helped me understand something that will be a critical point of this book: You have to realize that there is something special within you, a basic goodness that you must choose to manifest in every way you can—toward your family, your profession and your planet. *Each of us has something good to offer*.

I am convinced that all of us need to find and nurture our goodness to unlock the keys to achievement. By tapping into your goodness, you can make a difference on this earth. I believe you are born with the responsibility and the obligation to make a positive impact.

One of the most difficult aspects of adulthood is the fact that you have to balance fun with work and freedom with responsibilities. It is a task that life requires of us. And if we are wise, we take life's requirements as seriously as we take life's opportunities.

When you decide to pursue greatness, you are taking responsibility for your life. This means that you are choosing to accept the consequences of your actions, and to become the agent of your mental, physical, spiritual and material success. You may not always be able to control what life puts in your path, but I believe *you can always control who you are*.

Thanks to my mother and, later, Mr. Washington, I grew up with the subconscious conviction that I was going to be somebody, and because of that, there was not going to be room in my life for drugs, alcohol or criminal behavior. Many of those I grew up with foresaw no purpose in their lives. For them, there was no strength of conviction to empower them to resist the allure of drugs and alcohol and crime.

You know, when I relate stories from my early life, people often express amazement that I am not a recovering drug addict or alcoholic. I grew up around drug and alcohol abusers. I've seen people shoot up. Yet it never touched me. I cannot remember anyone even offering me drugs, at least not anyone who knew who I was.

Where many of my peers may have seen only a life in low-paying employment or life on the street, I dreamed of greatness. And those dreams propelled me to pursue greatness. As with my Mama and her desire to have a family, my consciousness became an active force.

## Radio Dreams

When Mr. Washington knighted me as a worthy young man, I felt free to dream again. He sent me out into the world on a quest for my destiny. Like many young people of my age, I belonged to the "Under the Pillow Club" of radio listeners who tuned in late at night when we were supposed to be asleep. Like most young people, I listened to rhythm and blues and, later, rock 'n' roll. But unlike many of my peers, I was as much entranced by the patter of the disc jockeys as by the beat of the music.

Listening to Miami's Pied Pipers of the radio, Milton "Butterball" Smith, Fred Hanna, King Coleman "The Bald-head Wonder," Nick with the Solid Kick, and Wild Man Steve, I decided I wanted to become a disc jockey, one of the platter-playin' papas, if you will.

I doubt that this profession was what Mr. Washington had in mind when he told me, "Open your mouth and you tell the world who you are," or when he lectured us on the power of the spoken word and the importance of developing our vocabularies. But I molded his meaning to my intent.

Eager to shake the label of special-education student, or of class dodo, I was propelled to the dictionary. I ran from Mr. Washington to Mr. Webster and set to memorizing as many impossibly impressive ten-dollar words as my mind could bear.

I read the dictionary every day and then practiced on my classmates. To this day, if you encounter my former schoolmates, they will describe me as the dude who mis-used a lot of big words, although truth be told, at the time neither they nor I knew enough to understand that I was abusing the language. I spoke the dictionary like a country boy speaks French. I mispronounced. I misappropriated. I mis-spent ten-dollar words in places where a nickel's worth would have paid the tab.

I called myself "Mister Vocabulary" and I developed a playground patter derived from the radio jocks who were my heroes. "Hey, they call me Mister Vocabulary. Linguistically or orationally, I'm emphatic that I possess an ad infinitum etymology which is simply unconquerable. However, I believe in the simplicity of life so without further ado, I want to be like Columbus and discover you."

Whenever I'd do my Mister Vocabulary rap at school, the fellows would holler, "GIVE ME FIVE, MY MAN!," and the girls would scream, "He's *BAD*, honey!" I thought I was *something*!

Despite my late-blooming enthusiasm for linguistics, I did not enroll in college. Instead, I continued to work toward my goal of becoming a radio disc jockey even while earning a daily wage as a city sanitation worker on Miami Beach. I also kept shadowing Mr. Washington, who worked with me on developing my speaking voice.

Eventually, my persistence paid off and I landed part-time work as a gofer at a local radio station in Miami, and I tried to absorb all I could by hanging out around the studio engineers and disc jockeys until the opportunity presented itself to get on the air, first as a fill-in deejay, and later as a full-time, bona fide disc jockey.

I was determined to get into broadcasting, and I set out to do it first by finding mentors who could prepare me for it, and then by wedging a foot in the door and worming my way to the microphone. When I set out, I had no idea how I would do it, but I knew life would present the opportunities if I was prepared and in a position to take advantage of them.

Educators and business leaders have said that the last few years have been the most difficult for young people and others in search of jobs. So many positions have been lost because of restructuring and downsizing in the workplace that the job market is tighter than it has been in decades. Even giants such as IBM have vowed to become leaner and meaner than ever before. I believe that opportunities still exist for those who are willing to get in the door and bide their time until openings appear.

## From Entertainer to Motivator

I sympathize and identify, however, with those who have been thrown out of their jobs because I was tossed out of broadcasting just as I felt I was closing in on my dream to become a nationally known disc jockey.

I had moved to a station in Columbus, Ohio, where I had a top-rated show. I was enjoying the fruits of my labors as a popular entertainer, but a friend, my long-time personal motivator, Mike Williams, counseled that perhaps there was a greater use for my talents. Mike, who worked as the station's news director, had a greater vision for me than I had for myself. He believed that I could become a voice for good, rather than simply a voice for good times.

With his encouragement, I found myself becoming more and more of a social commentator and community activist, urging my listeners to make something of themselves and to address problems in their neighborhoods with political action.

And then I found myself on the street. The owners of the station felt I had become too controversial. They fired me. It was a depressing, challenging time, but the Mamie Brown in me manifested itself.

Anytime my mother suffered a setback or disappointment, she put her head down and plowed ahead. I tapped into that history and began to transform the negatives into positive energy. I followed her example.

Being controversial definitely had its drawbacks, but it also brought notoriety of the sort that politicians crave: name recognition. And when a friend named Horace Perkins suggested that political office might be a logical next step for someone who had been a community activist, I agreed to think it over. After some initial skepticism about my suitability for public office, I became convinced that I could rise to the task.

I had picked up confidence in myself by that stage in my life and I liked to take on challenges. I believe that you can do things you never imagined if you challenge yourself. I began researching the political arena. I observed the legislature in session. I prepared myself for a campaign just as I had prepped for a broadcasting career. I focused my energy through force of will and consciousness. I listened and I learned and I said, "I know I can do this."

I beat the incumbent in the Twenty-ninth House District. In my first term, I introduced and passed more legislation than any other freshman legislator in the history of the state. In my third term, I served as chairman of the Human Resource Committee.

## Mama Falls Ill

I served three terms as an Ohio state representative and I was entertaining thoughts of running for the state senate when a crisis arose. My mother became sick with food poisoning, a severe case that nearly took her life. It was the only time she'd ever been hospitalized. She needed constant supervision and I felt I was the one to provide it.

It was not much of a decision on my part. I had to be with her and help her through it. My mother had a low tolerance for the winters of Ohio, so I resigned from public office and moved back to Liberty City to care for her. I was concerned about supporting myself and those dependent upon me, but I knew that I owed whatever I had become and would become to my Mama.

You have to look at what you value most. I was in a position of leadership and considerable power in the legislature, but the people who find it hard to give up that kind of power are those who identify too closely with it.

I don't define myself by titles. In the legislature, I had a friend who insisted that he be called "Senator," as if he was born with that name. Having the title of state legislator was no big thing to me. Being the son of Mrs. Mamie Brown is far more important than that.

To this day, there are people who are astonished that I would walk away from a position that I had worked so hard to attain. But I cannot understand why they don't understand. I liked my job. I love my mother.

While with Mama back in Liberty City, I became involved in community affairs. I was given a city contract to do career training for young people in Liberty City. And, again, I became something of a controversial figure because I spoke out against injustice and for heightened political awareness in the city of Miami. As a guest editorial speaker on a local radio station, I called for people to register to vote and exercise their power. The registration drive resulted in four thousand new voters at the polls and the largest turnout in the city's history. I organized what the newspapers called "the largest peaceful demonstration in Miami since the 1960's."

When I spoke out against what I perceived to be an injustice, people listened. Some of them liked what I had to say; others did not. And because of my outspokenness, I found myself under investigation by the Dade County state's attorney, Janet Reno.

When I stepped forward as a community spokesman, I was targeted. An investigation was begun into the youth program I was operating. There were many news stories about it. The investigation was a farce, but while it went on, I couldn't go anywhere either. My life was on hold.

There were no news stories about my vigil at the state's attorney's office. For an entire year, I went down every day and stood outside her office with a sign around my neck. It said: INDICT ME OR SET ME FREE! IF YOU HAVE SOMETHING AGAINST ME THAT I HAVE DONE WRONG, PROSECUTE ME TO THE FULL EXTENT OF THE LAW. IF NOT, GET OFF MY BACK.

As a native of The Alley, I did not take personal attacks lying down. I knew this investigation was no more than a smear campaign. I had done nothing wrong other than dare

to speak out in a neighborhood with few strong voices. It
irked me when some of my neighbors said, "You're gonna
make the state's attorney mad!"

"Make *her* mad? *I'm* mad!" I would reply.

I was outraged, and so every morning when Janet Reno
stepped off the elevator, I would say, "Good morning, Janet!" I'd have a big smile on my face.

She and her assistants probably thought I was a crazy
man. They weren't too far off at that point. I was crazed at
the idea of what they were dragging me through. And I was
not the only one upset. Eventually, even those who didn't
agree with me or sympathize with me began to say that it
was unfair to keep open an investigation that had no merit.

Public support forced Reno to drop the investigation.
The only thing they found wrong with my program was
"sloppy bookkeeping." Otherwise, I was exonerated, but
only after living under a cloud of allegations for a year. In
the end, they did uncover this startling revelation: I had
actually spent $13,000 of my own money to subsidize the
program.

My name had been dragged through the mud and I was
weary, but you know the old saying—"Tough times don't
last, tough people do."

## Motivational Career

I endured. After I was vindicated, the city offered me another $100,000 to continue the program in Liberty City but
I had decided to move on with my life. I had long been
interested in the impact of motivational and professional
speakers and their ability to invest people with a purpose
and goals for their lives. I decided to pursue that dream.

Just as I had done with broadcasting and politics, I im-
mersed myself in that world. It did not come without a cost.

To work on my public-speaking career, I moved to Detroit, where I had made some contacts in the field. At one point, I had to beg the owner of my office building there to give me three months' free rent so I could hold on to my office space.

I didn't tell him then, but I was also living in that office space because I could not afford to rent an apartment. But after years of training and working on my speaking career, I now pay the rent. Today, I speak around the country to *Fortune* 500 companies as well as to groups of young people. Public-television stations around the country broadcast my speeches during fund-raising drives, and they tell me that I inspire their listeners to contribute more than any other speaker.

When I started out, I made extra money by selling cassette tapes of my speeches for ten dollars. They were home-made copies, wrapped in rubber bands. Last year, my company, Les Brown Unlimited, took in more than a million dollars in speaking fees and from the sale of my videotapes and audiotapes. I am grateful for that, but my goal in life and in these pages is to do more than build financial security.

I have a gift, a humble one that I have labored greatly to develop and refine as a force for good. My dream is to inspire you to enlarge your vision of yourself, to develop *your* gifts and in turn inspire others, particularly young people, so that we may all work not just to better ourselves but to better our world.

## Nine Principles of Life Enrichment

I offer you these nine principles of life enrichment, which will be explored in the following pages:

I.   I can achieve far beyond my horizons, and in avenues of life I have never explored.

II.  I possess a basic goodness, which is the foundation for the greatness I can ultimately achieve.

III.  I must take responsibility for my actions, my well-being and the attainment of my maximum potential.

IV.  I must seek self-awareness, self-approval and self-commitment in order to attain self-fulfillment.

V.  I must commit myself to building and maintaining relationships that are critical to the social development of my family and community.

VI.  I must manifest the belief that mutual respect is the fundamental element of all relationships.

VII.  I will heighten my life by helping others heighten theirs.

VIII.  I will work toward my goals by planning, executing and measuring my progress.

IX.  I will make commitments with care and honor them with integrity.

I offer you these principles for your consideration and guidance, and in this book I also offer lessons from my life as testimony that you can live your dreams. I would particularly like to emphasize that with the gifts you have been given comes the responsibility to use and develop them.

As a result of my own experiences, I believe you can accomplish almost anything you want in any arena if you focus the power at your disposal. If you put yourself in a position where you have to *stretch outside your comfort zone*, then you are forced to expand your consciousness and to strive and achieve. Those powers may be dormant within you but they exist. I know. I've been there. I'll wager that *there is more in you than you are now expressing.*

Can you imagine looking back on your life and discovering that you have used so few of your natural gifts? Henry David Thoreau said, "Oh, God, to reach the point of death only to realize you have never lived."

It is a frightening thought, isn't it? To know that your dreams may die with you rather than blossom during your lifetime. You know, most people go to their graves without doing that, so their epitaphs could read: "Dead but not used up." I want life to use me up, and I hope that is your decision too.

I hope you don't take anything with you to the grave, that you use up all the gifts that you were given so that they remain on this planet when you are gone, enriching it for all who follow.

As the son of Mrs. Mamie Brown, I have a particularly strong motivation to use my gifts. You see, if I don't make use of my gift, my Mama has threatened to call the great Repo Man in the sky.

## My Mother's Gift

Diphtheria swept through my neighborhood when I was a small boy and it took many lives, including that of my little buddy, a boy everyone called "Gramps." He and I contracted it about the same time and we became backyard buddies; we played together because no one else would for fear of contracting what we had.

When Gramps's condition worsened, his mother got enough money together so that she could afford to take him to the hospital. He died there. It was my first exposure to the death of someone my own age. I had thought only old people died. I could not understand why Gramps would die, especially since, at the wake, he looked to be just asleep.

With the death of Gramps and several other neighborhood children, my mother became extremely protective of me. She was determined not to lose me. She refused to put me in the hospital because Gramps had died there. She talked the doctors into giving her the expensive medicine so that she could administer it herself. I can still envision how her hands shook when she gave it to me because she was so fearful of wasting any of it.

Mama did not sleep much during my illness but one night when she had gone to her own room to get some rest, I awoke to see a figure at the end of my bed. I recognized Miss Henry, an elderly neighbor whom I had often visited before her death several months earlier. Miss Henry loved me. I would sit by her bedside for hours and talk to her.

When I saw that it was Miss Henry who had come to my bedside, I yelled for my Mama. "Mama! Miss Henry is in my room!" Mama came running. She was angry. My Mama believed in stories of dead people who come back to try to take loved ones with them. After nursing me along, she surely was not going to let Miss Henry get me.

Mama came storming into the room cursing, "If she ain't dead yet, she soon will be!"

I had NO idea how Mama was going to kill Miss Henry AGAIN! But Mama didn't get the chance. When she came into the room and turned the light on, Miss Henry disappeared.

Mama kept cursing just in case she was hanging around somewhere. "Don't you come in here ever again messin' with my boy!" Mama said. "Stay outta this house!"

After her cursing wore down, Mama went to praying at my bedside and apparently the prayers did their work. In the next few days, the diphtheria began to release its hold on me.

Then, just as it appeared that I was recovering, I came to her one morning after awakening and my voice was gone. Mama was devastated. After all she had gone through in dealing with my illness, she feared it had sneaked back in and robbed me of my voice forever.

That night, she set to praying again, "Lord, give the child my voice. I've talked enough in my life. I don't need my voice no more."

In the morning, I awakened and I called to my mother. My voice had returned. My Mama said, "Thank God!"

Or she tried to say that. Her voice was nothing but a squeak. I swear it is true.

She went to the medicine cabinet and took some of my diphtheria medicine herself, and in a few hours her voice returned. But always after that, if I sassed my mother or she heard me curse, she reminded me of that time.

She would say, "You talk like that again, I'll *take* my voice back. I asked Jesus to give you my voice and he did. You use it like that, I'll take it back.

"You know *Jesus does what I ask of him!*"

I intend to use my Mama's voice for good, lest I lose it for good. I urge you to use your talents and gifts to their fullest too.

[See exercises for this chapter in the Action Planner on page 233.]

# Two

# *You Gotta Be Hungry!*

*Press on. Nothing can take the place of persistence. Talent will not; the world is full of unsuccessful people with talent. Genius will not; unrewarded genius is almost a proverb. Education alone will not; the world is full of educated derelicts. Persistence and determination alone are omnipotent.*

—CALVIN COOLIDGE

One of the worst-kept secrets in my old neighborhood was that young Les Brown was a heavy load upon his poor Mama. It was true. I was a *mischievous* boy.

I would not come in for dinner. I'd climb under moving railroad cars and swim in abandoned rock pits. I'd play checkers with the old men and talk a lot of trash to them. I'd sneak with my buddy Bou under the fence at the Canada Dry distributors and swipe bottles of ginger ale.

And in school I was the class clown. School was boring to me and the more boring it got, the more mischievous I became. I released pigeons during assembly. I threw food in the cafeteria. I was always in the principal's office and they were always calling Mama in.

## Seat of the Pants Psychology

At one point, she told me that if they dragged her down to that school again she was going to take a frying pan to my head. That got my attention. For a while at least. You see, Mama hadn't heard about using psychology to get to the problems locked in a child's subconscious mind. She seemed to believe that the problems were locked in my *behind*, and she was determined to beat them out of me like dust out of a rug.

Mama was not completely out of step with modern behavioral psychology, however. For instance, when I did something to anger her and she beat my behind, she would say positive affirmations such as "You goin' to *be* somethin'. There ain't nothin' wrong with you. A hard head makes for a *soft* behind!"

My mother believed that I would amount to something someday, but hers was certainly not the majority opinion in the neighborhood. All through my youth I heard people— particularly Miss Catherine, our nosy, snuff-dipping neighbor—tell my mother that I was never going to amount to anything. Miss Catherine got on my *last* nerve. Whenever I'd get in trouble she'd come over and say, *"Mamie, take him back to the Welfare Department."*

But my Mama, bless her, didn't listen. Her friends and many of my teachers may have told my mother differently, but she believed that I would become someone worthwhile and she made me believe it too. And now when life knocks me down I say, "Life, I am getting back up because I want to make my Mama proud of me! I'm getting back up because all of my life I have been told I would be a loser. They said I wouldn't make it so I'm gonna SHOW them that I CAN!"

I believe that when life knocks you down you should always try to land on your back because *if you can look up, you can get up!* I get up to prove those people wrong and to prove that Mama was right in taking me in and keeping me when they told her to send me back. I have that *hunger* within to make something of myself. That hunger is my *motivating force*.

*Wanting* something is not enough. You must *hunger* for it. Your motivation must be absolutely compelling. You may not need the threat of a frying pan to your head or a tree switch to your behind, but we all need some form of deeply rooted, powerful motivation. It empowers us to overcome obstacles so that we can live our dreams.


## A Drive to Achieve

I flew back to Columbus, Ohio, to give a speech recently, and I ran into a very hungry young man, one of those people whose attitude and energy tell you that he will be somebody—that success is inevitable for this person.

I had spoken at a breakfast gathering in Columbus, and afterward I'd had a meeting at the airport. The meeting had run long, and I'd missed my plane. I was walking to the ticket counter to get a new ticket when this young man approached me.

"I'd like to talk with you, Mr. Brown," he said. "A friend of mine told me that you could help me go to Morehouse College."

Now, when I was a radio commentator in Columbus, I developed a reputation as someone who could help young people accomplish their goals. Often, I would help them connect with someone in a position to provide the assistance they needed.

"Why do you want to go to Morehouse?" I asked.

"I want to be a minister, sir," he replied, "and that is where Dr. Martin Luther King went to school. Morehouse has a reputation for developing great orators and ministers. But it costs nine thousand dollars and I have only fifteen hundred."

As he spoke, a question came to mind. *How had this young man found me?* I asked him.

"Well, I knew you were in town for a speech, but I couldn't afford a ticket to get in," he said. "I knew you would have to leave sometime from the airport, so I've been out here all day walking from gate to gate, looking for you."

This was a hungry young man! What powerful motivation this young man had! What determination to walk around the airport all day looking for me. He had no idea what time my flight would be leaving. There was no doubt in my mind I was *meant* to miss my plane so that this young man would find me. Somebody said, "Coincidences are God's way of staying anonymous."

"Young man," I said, "*it's done*. When you have that kind of determination, you won't be denied. I may not be able to get you into Morehouse personally, but with your determination and my contacts, we will be hard to stop!"

This young man is the sort of person whose determination will not allow him to be denied his dreams and goals.

## Too Legit to Quit

When people have that kind of motivation, when obstacles are not a factor, when only the *dream* matters, they MAKE things happen. The universe has no choice but to yield to that sort of energy. Such people are virtually *unstoppable*. They are, as rapper M. C. Hammer says, "Too legit to quit."

Remember Buster Douglas, the unknown fighter from Columbus, Ohio, who beat heavyweight champion Mike Tyson? Well, in his fight with Tyson, Douglas was knocked down hard. Lying on that canvas, he was a man with powerful motivation to get up. At that point, Douglas was being beaten up by life in general. He was on the verge of becoming a bum. He had only recently been released from an alcohol recovery center. His mother had died. Someone close to him had a terminal illness. He got up because he was determined to prove that he was not a bum. He got up, and he won because of the deeply rooted power of his motivation. It came up from down deep.

Douglas became the heavyweight champion, and then he had to defend HIS title against all challengers. The first—and last—was Evander Holyfield. The Buster Douglas who fought in this match was a different man. As champion, he had a guaranteed purse of $24 million *even if he lost* to Holyfield. His motivation in the second fight with Holyfield was a great deal less than when he was fighting for his survival in that first match with Tyson.

Buster lost that second fight. I believe that you have to have a *powerful* reason to get up and fight back in life. That is why you must find a powerful motivation to drive you. It has to matter *deeply;* otherwise, you may not have the strength of purpose to persevere.

I asked a friend recently why he was not working on his dream to have his own business. He said that by the time he got through working sixty-five hours a week he didn't have enough energy left to act on his goal. He had put it aside.

He is not alone. There have been numerous studies and reports indicating that Americans are working longer hours, enjoying their work less and living in fear that they might lose their jobs any day. If you live like that, you need to stoke the fires of your hunger. That's not living!

Feeding a fire within you—living FOR a dream—is REAL living. In the course of my conversation with this friend, I got him thinking about his dream of having his own restaurant. I added some coals to his fires. I fanned them too. His hunger was rekindled because he realized that starting his own business was the way to get off the treadmill.

Life does not always present us with an ideal situation in which to pursue our dreams. That is where HUNGER comes in. We must motivate ourselves to do what we MUST do to get on and go on with our lives.

My friend is still working those long sixty-five-hour weeks, but he has found the time to go after his dream. He is *hungry* again, so he goes deep within and finds the strength to stay after it. He focuses on his goal. He stays motivated by remembering his dream. He has his life in gear again and his dream back in his sights.

## Drive, Survive and Thrive!

Have you ever had the experience of getting in your car, starting it up, pushing the accelerator to the floor to back out of the driveway—and the car doesn't move? Then you realize you've got the emergency brake on and you release it and the car just glides out.

Well, many of us go through life with the brakes on. The brakes of fear, the brakes of procrastination, the brakes of unworthiness, the brakes of negative thinking. These prevent us from giving all that we have to give and sharing all that we have to share. You cannot live as though you have a thousand years to accomplish your goals. You are here today, but you may be gone tomorrow. Maybe even gone *today*. It is necessary that you follow your dream TODAY.

One day I talked on the phone about a project to a very creative person. Marion was her name. The next day her husband called to say she had dropped dead. I went to visit her husband the day before her funeral and I helped him go through all of her unfinished dreams. It was one of the saddest things I have ever had to do. Marion had great talent but she was insecure about it and those insecurities kept her talents from flourishing.

Marion had written so many things that were never completed or published. All of these bits of her life were just lying about her office, unfinished and unshared. She had wonderful stories and profound poems strewn about the house. I remember a play that she had talked of writing. I found notes on it, but she had never sat down and done it. And so it will *never* be written. We all lost out because Marion's talent was unfulfilled. Marion's writing might have inspired you or me to greater accomplishments or greater understanding. But not now.

How much time do you have left? You don't know. Marion didn't know either. Now she is gone and she has taken her greatness and talents and abilities to the grave with her. Develop hunger and the sense that you have to *use up* your time on this planet. Use what you've got. Share whatever you brought into this life.

When you get discouraged—and you will—it takes hunger to develop the courage to try again and again and never quit. Some people are *naturally* hungry. Some have hunger imposed upon them by circumstances. If you are not naturally motivated, you are going to have to learn how to make yourself hungry. I can help. I'm a GOOD cook.

## Cooking Up Hunger

To help you build hunger, I suggest you try these steps:

• Develop hunger by taking responsibility for your life. Know that it is up to you to accomplish your dreams. Get the feel for this at first by setting small goals and accomplishing them. Set a goal of walking, jogging or riding a bicycle for a half hour every other day. Do it for a week and then increase the time. Feel the satisfaction it gives you and notice the effect it has on your weight and your overall sense of self-control and self-approval. Nobody cares as much about you and your dream as you do.

• Review your goals twice every day. Be focused on achieving them. Reflect on what truly motivates you.

• Develop a sense of urgency in your life. Take actions now that will move you toward your goals. If you want to change jobs, put your résumé together today and mail it out to a company you would like to work for. Isn't that a satisfying feeling? Just taking an action like that makes you feel better about yourself.

• Develop courage. Let yourself feel the fears that are holding you back and mentally push them aside. Afraid of water? Enroll in swimming lessons now. Master that fear. Remember the Cowardly Lion in *The Wizard of Oz*? He sang a song to overcome his fears. COURAGE!

• Devote yourself to operating on a massive, relentless scale in order to accomplish your goals. Instead of making ten sales calls, make fifty and watch the rewards come in.

• Develop the conviction that you can accomplish your goal. Your level of belief in yourself will inevitably manifest itself in what you do.

• Read inspirational material such as the biographies of people who overcame great odds to succeed. If they can do it, you can do it.

• Tap into your spiritual awareness and contemplate your mortality. Write your obituary and predict your accomplishments at the end of life. Are you satisfied with what you put down? There are few motivations as compelling as the concept that sooner or later death awaits you. If possible, talk with elderly people who are close to you. Gently ask them what things they wish they had accomplished. No one wants to die with his or her potential unfulfilled.

• Get acquainted with successful people and ask what drives them and how they achieve their goals. You will be surprised at how flattered they will be by your attention. Listen to their ideas and experiences. Make them your role models.

• Develop your communications skills. Take public-speaking courses or courses on leadership and communication. We live in a society in which these skills are perhaps the most important of all.

• SMILE! Project a positive image. Say "YES!" to your life. A person's smile reflects how he or she feels inside. Your smile will give you a positive countenance that will make people feel comfortable around you. Did you know that the muscles that create a smile trigger a chemical in the brain that makes you feel good all over? So SMILE! Feel *GOOD* about your dreams!

## Demons of Distraction

It is important that while you pursue your goals you tune out distractions and self-defeating thoughts. Let your hunger for your goals propel you on a dead-ahead course. I had a goal of losing some weight because my blood-pressure level was up and my cholesterol level was high. When I'm on a diet—or as I prefer to say, "When I am managing my food choices"—those little diet demons try to take control and sidetrack me.

And all too often, I'm ashamed to say, I give in to them! I am weak in the presence of edible temptation. I'm the kind of guy who very carefully peels all the skin off his fried chicken, but then I eat the chicken and the skin too! Those diet demons are devious.

I really do have to work on my motivation for dieting. I thought I had it going not long ago when I saw a performance of the Alvin Ailey Dancers. I saw the way women reacted to those guys up there onstage with their washboard stomachs and I decided I was going to have a washboard stomach too.

After seeing all those women in the audience making eyes at those skinny guys, I was MOTIVATED. I went to a fancy sporting-goods and fitness store and bought myself the best jogging suit they had. I bought some of the best workout shoes. I topped my fitness outfit off with a state-of-the-art orthopedically approved, ergonomically correct sit-up board.

To make sure I made good use of that sit-up board, I put it right beside my bed so that I could roll out of bed and right onto it and do my three sets of fifty repetitions first thing every morning.

*But it didn't work!* My stomach got fatter instead of flatter! It looked more like an *outboard* than a *washboard*. So I put the sit-up board back into the box and took it right back to the fitness emporium.

I walked up to the salesman and said, "I want my money back; this sit-up board did not work."

He looked at the board. He looked at me. He looked at my stomach.

"Did you even get on it?" he asked.

"Yes, every day, and it didn't work at all," I said.

"Well, we have never had this happen before," the sales clerk said.

And I got my money back.

That poor sales clerk. I told him the truth. He just didn't ask me the right question.

You see, I did get on that sit-up board every morning. He *should* have asked me what I *did* when I got on it.

I ATE ON IT! Buttered pancakes and sweet rolls in the morning! Some sweet-potato pie at bedtime!

Oh, those diet demons. Every time I try to lose weight they remind me of a story I read one time. They say, "A skinny guy was hit by a truck and killed. If he'd had a little more weight, he might have lived. So have a bucket of chicken. Have a barrel of fun, Les!" And I DO!

That distracting inner voice can be awesome, but if you have *true* hunger you can stand up to it—although you may have to stoke that hunger every day with little pep talks about the importance of your goals. I do that by writing down my most vital goals—obviously, getting in shape is not yet on the list—and reading them every morning when I get up and again at night right before I go to bed. That builds strong hunger.

After I get up in the morning and review my goals I start

writing out ideas. (When you are hungry for your dreams, you have to get up REAL early to get everything done.) I jot down ideas that might enable me to reach my goals and I try not to judge their merits too much at first. I just write first and evaluate later. Sometimes I write fifteen or twenty. Some days it is more difficult than others. (Some days, my most powerful idea is to stay in bed and sleep a couple more hours.) But I get up because I know that *one idea can change your life*.

With a powerful hunger for your dreams driving you, you will be surprised at the ideas that will come, at the people you will be able to attract, at the opportunities that will unfold. You will be able to see things that you won't believe you couldn't see before—things that may have been there right in front of you the whole time.

## *One Idea That Really Stuck*

A rt Fry had a problem while singing in the North Presbyterian Church choir. He kept losing his place in the choir book because his bookmark kept slipping down into the book. Because his bookmark disappeared, Art was left to fumble through the pages when it came time to sing.

Now, Art had worked his way through the University of Minnesota by selling pots and pans door-to-door. He had always had a knack for inventing things as a child, and after he earned a degree in chemical engineering, he landed a job as a product-development specialist at 3M Corporation in Rochester, Minnesota. He was the perfect man to ponder the eternal question of "bookmark droop."

And so he did. He came up with a bookmark that had a bit of stickum on it. The idea stuck so well, in fact, that Art looked for other applications. He decided his sticky bookmark would make a great little memo pad. At first most of his co-workers thought Art had been inhaling glue fumes too long. But then Art began giving out his sticky little notepads, and one day, when one of his top bosses walked through the snow for several blocks just to get some more, Art knew his Post-its were a great idea!

Art's idea became one of the top-selling office products in 3M's inventory. It earns his company millions of dollars each year. And Art has risen to the high-paying and esteemed position of 3M corporate scientist. He now spends his days looking for more good ideas because 3M knows the power of a single idea.

*Get your ideas on paper and study them. Don't let them go to waste!*

## A Hungry Person Is Never Dis-couraged for Long

Hunger gives you the courage to take your ideas and run with them. Hunger helps you overcome discourage-ment; it moves you to use up your talents and your life. When I was a boy, I sold used television sets door to-door in my neighborhood with my buddy Bou. (His nickname came from a French-speaking neighbor who saw him as a baby and pronounced him *très beau*—"very beautiful.")

Bou and I discovered that selling door-do-door can be cruel and unusual punishment. I'd go up to a door, knock on it, and politely say, "Hello, would you like to buy a nice *working* television set?"

"NO!" And the door would slam in my face. BAM!

The first time Bou had that happen, he headed back to his car. "*I can't do this,*" he said.

But I *couldn't* go back to the car. My Mama was ill at that time. She couldn't work. I was hungry, *literally* hungry.

I couldn't afford to quit, so I kept going. That's a powerful motivation. I've known people who have deliberately put themselves in a "can't afford to quit" position just to make sure they stay on the track to their goals.

I discovered back then on the door-to-door route that when you step into your fears and continue to push yourself, something happens to you. You develop courage.

I kept on. From one door to the next.

No! Bam!

No! Bam!

No! Bam!

You know what? After a while, I no longer took it personally. I began to play a game. I thought there must be a "Yes" out there somewhere and I decided that I wasn't going home until I found one.

And eventually somebody did say "Yes!" and I said, "I *knew* I would find you."


## Driving That Hard and Lonely Road

If you don't develop the hunger and courage to pursue your goal, you will lose your nerve and you will give up on your dream. If you don't have the courage to act, life will take the initiative from you. Act on life or risk having life act on YOU.

Remember that song that went "If it ain't one thing it's another. . . ."? Someone once told me that we are either in a problem, just leaving one or headed for one. To overcome the tough times in life and actively pursue your goals, you need to nurture a hunger that refuses to be denied. Hunger will get you through the hard times when you will want to give up. You are going to be visited by Mr. Murphy of Murphy's Law, the one that says, *"Anything that can go wrong will go wrong and at the worst possible moment."*

When Mr. Murphy comes knocking, and he will, you may look at all of my tapes and this book and want to put

them in the trash can, set them afire and stomp on the ashes.
At times you will grit your teeth, clench your fists and say,
"If I could just find that Les Brown . . ."

No matter what I tell you, nothing will protect you from
the nasty side of life. It will catch you on the blind side, drop
you to your knees and choke you. People will betray you. It
is going to happen. They will lie to you. That will happen
too. Someone will say, "Oh, you can count on me," and then
not show up. Remember this: "The most dependable hand
you can rely on is the one at the end of your wrist." You
can't count on anyone but yourself.

When I was a state representative, I once had a special
piece of legislation I was eager to have approved. I approached a fellow member of the House and I said, "Look,
can I count on your vote?" He said, "Yes." I asked if he was
certain he would support me, because there was another
fellow I could call upon if he didn't feel comfortable supporting the bill. He assured me I could count on him.

The legislation came up and he voted against my bill. I
went to him and said, "You told me you would vote for my
legislation."

"I lied," he said.

HE LIED! I was shocked.

But that's life. Be prepared for it. Have your hunger fired
and ready.

To persevere in hard times, you will have to call on your
deepest purpose. Sometimes yours will be a lonely journey.
Know that not everyone will support you. Sometimes the
individuals you thought would serve as your *en*couragers,
turn out to be your *dis*couragers. When I decided to act upon
my dream to become a public speaker I quit my job in the
appliance department of a big store in order to devote all of
my energy to pursuing my goal. I thought my mother would
admire my hunger. Instead, my Mama said, "Les, you had
a *good* job at Sears. That man there liked you."

I said, "Mama, I can't go back to Sears. I've got to be my
own boss. This is my life. I *have* to do this."

My Mama just couldn't see it for me. You have to know what is right for you, and go after it regardless of what others say. Others judge you based on what they have seen you do. You must operate on the basis of your *vision* for yourself. Nobody is going to care more about your goals than you. Nobody is going to put more time in on them than you. You have to find your own source of hunger and motivation and let it drive you.

## Motivation by Fire

There was once a Roman general who realized this as he was about to send his reluctant troops into a battle in which they were greatly outnumbered. The general knew his men would have to be highly motivated to win and they weren't. So, after his army had sailed to the enemy's land and disembarked on the hostile shore, he gave the order for his OWN ships to be burned. The general then commanded his troops, "We win, or we die!" With that *strong* motivation, they won.

To build hunger, develop a "do-or-die" attitude. Burn your ships if you have to. On the job, do more than you are paid for. Develop the habit of setting standards that others will measure themselves by. Make this your motto: *"Do not go where the path may lead, but go where there is no path, and leave a trail."*

A friend in sales told me he was in trouble financially because his business was down. I asked him how many phone calls he was making a day. He said "Twenty-five."

I said, "Double them. Make fifty. Or seventy-five. Or one hundred."

He said, "Aw, man, that's too much."

"Too MUCH! You tell me that you are behind on your bills and then you say it's too much? You know, one way to get back on your feet real quick is to miss two car payments. How can you say anything is too much when you have everything at stake?"

When I began looking for work as a speaker, I developed a callus on my ear that is still there. I made so many telephone calls I got *call-i-flower* ears. If anyone got within three feet of me, I went after their business. I believed the name of the game was TTP: *Talk To People*. If that didn't work I tried another game—TTMP: *Talk To More People*.

You would be surprised how well that sort of dynamic approach pays off. It may take a few weeks or months but it works. I handed out a business card to someone and it was three years later when he found the card in some old papers and called me to do business. I landed another big account when a man I'd never met found one of my tapes on a desk in someone else's office. *You have to get your material out there on a massive scale.* Consider it your personal crusade. Your life's mission.

You don't have to tell truly HUNGRY people to do their homework or to set high standards or to go at it massively. They realize those are essential steps in reaching their goals. People bound for greatness jump out of bed and embrace the morning.

## A Hunger for Real Estate

Eula McClaney, a sharecropper's daughter from Orion, Alabama, was so poor that she was still working behind the plow at age twenty-six. Then she married and moved to Pittsburgh and had two daughters. When her children were old enough to go to school, she decided that she wanted to go to work to improve the family's life. But her husband, a steelworker, adamantly opposed the idea.

He did not share her visions of a better life. Following a

persistent voice that told her to strike out on her own, Eula began working extra jobs. She did housecleaning, baby-sat for other children and sold her homemade sweet-potato pies. Her goal was to own property. She would raise the down payments to buy homes and business property and then rent them out to make the monthly payments and a slight profit.

Often, the properties needed work, but her husband refused to join her in the business. Within a few years, Eula had built up a small fortune. She owned and managed nearly forty properties. She bought a Rolls-Royce and a twelve-room house in a prestigious neighborhood. Her husband refused to live there, so she lived there with her daughters and other relatives.

Her success in real estate eventually inspired Eula to move to California, the hottest real-estate market in the country. When she suggested that her husband move with her he refused. He was comfortable with the status quo, but she wanted more and she didn't mind taking chances to get it.

She took her daughters to Los Angeles. She bought a hotel in California and had hardly settled in when her husband notified her by mail that he had filed for divorce. She lost much of her hard-earned money in the divorce, but this incredible woman persevered in her dream.

She became immensely wealthy in the California real-estate boom. I learned of her from a segment on *Lifestyles of the Rich and Famous*. I was inspired to meet her and hear her story. And when I did meet her, she told me that at one point she had prayed on her knees, "Lord, what can I do to help my husband share my vision of a better future?"

She said the reply came to her clearly, *"Do it yourself."* She did, and she later wrote a book titled *God, I Listened*. Before her death, she donated millions to education, to the American Cancer Society and to the American Heart Association. In all, she bequeathed $30 million to charities—one tenth of her estate.

She once told me, "Many times I wanted to give up. Many times I did not know where I was going to get my next meal. Many times I wanted to call my husband and say, 'Baby, you were right; can we come back home?' But during those times, there was also something inside me that told me not to give up, to just keep on keeping on. I decided that I would not stop. And I made it happen."

Find that voice in yourself. Look deep into yourself for it. If others don't hear it, that's okay. It is there in you. It is there in all of us. We all have a driving force within us. Keep in mind that when you hear those encouraging voices, you must listen to them and ignore all logic. Mere logic does not always work.

## Logic Doesn't Always Make Sense

Think about it. For hundreds of years, logical, reasonable thinking caused man to walk and ride on the backs of animals and view himself as capable of traveling solely by land or by water. Logical thinking said, *"Man, you can't fly. If God had wanted man to fly he would have given you wings. He gave wings to birds. Birds fly. Man, you are a FOOL to dream that you could join the birds."* Fortunately, Orville and Wilbur Wright were deaf to such logic.

In moments of self-doubt, you can always build a logical case as to why you can't accomplish your goal. And your logical friends will chime in with their negative but well-reasoned, perfectly logical assessments. Remember this: The limitations you have and the negative things you internalize have been given to you by the world. The things that will EMPOWER you are those that you give yourself.

I remember a football game when Florida A&M University was down by thirty points and the team's coach, Jake Gaither, came on the public-address system and said in his booming bass-drum voice, "The Rattlers will strike again, and again. And again. And again. And again and AGAIN! We will NEVER give up!"

That is how you must attack your goals. Never, never, never give up.

As a young man just out of high school in Florida, I worked for the sanitation department on Miami Beach, but my dream was to be a radio disc jockey. So I started working on my communications skills and expanding my vocabulary.

I envisioned myself on the air, having my own show, talking and playing records. I envisioned people listening to me. That was my vision. That was my dream. I held it in my mind constantly.

My mentor in high school was my teacher Mr. Washington, the man who would teach me not to live within other people's labels of me as educable mentally retarded. Mr. Washington often repeated a quote from the late civil-rights leader Whitney Young, Jr.: "It is better to be prepared for an opportunity and not have one *than to have an opportunity and not be prepared.*"

And so I began preparing myself to go on the radio. I practiced all the time. Practice, practice, practice. By the way, practice does not make perfect. Banish that belief from your brain. Perfection does not exist. You can always do better. You can always grow. Otherwise, why are you here? *Practice only makes for improvement.*

## Hungry for Airtime

So, to become a radio disc jockey, I practiced and practiced to improve. I worked on my delivery and technical skills every day for weeks and weeks. And finally I went to the radio station that I had targeted in Miami, and I asked for the program director, Mr. Milton "Butterball" Smith.

I had to go down there during my lunch break from my mowing job, and old Butterball looked at my overalls and my straw hat and said, "Do you have any radio experience?"

"No, sir, I don't," I said.

"Do you have any journalism background?"

"No, sir, I don't," I replied. "But I can never get it if you don't give me the opportunity. I've been practicing a lot, sir."

"I'm sorry," he said. "We don't have a job for you."

I thanked him and left. But I was not defeated. You see, he did not know my purpose for being there. I wanted to become a disc jockey, yes, but my deeper purpose was to buy my mother a house. I had a big dream for a grass cutter. But I also had a big hunger.

My favorite program on television back then was *The Millionaire*. It was the show in which the central character, Michael Anthony, would search someone out and present that person each week with a check for one million dollars.

That was my fantasy, to get a million dollars so I could buy my mother one of those big homes on Miami Beach. And so, after Butterball rolled right over me, I went back and talked with Mr. Washington. He told me not to take it personally. He said some people are so negative they have to say no seven times before they say yes.

He told me to go back to Butterball. So the next day I went back to the station and said "Hello, Mr. Butterball, how are you doing? My name is Les Brown."

"I know your name," he replied. "Didn't I just see you here yesterday?"

"Yes, sir," I said. "Do you have any jobs here?"

"Didn't I just tell you yesterday that we didn't have any jobs?" he said.

"Yes, sir," I responded, "but I thought maybe someone got fired or resigned."

"Nobody resigned or got fired," Butterball said. "We don't have any jobs."

I thanked him politely and left.

And the next day, I was back, acting as though I was seeing him for the first time.

"How are you doing, Mr. Butterball?"

"What do you want now, young man? I'm busy."

I asked if he had any jobs available.

"Didn't I just tell you yesterday and the day before that we didn't have any jobs?" he replied.

"I didn't know, sir," I said. "I thought maybe somebody died."

"NO ONE DIED. NO ONE GOT FIRED. NO ONE GOT LAID OFF. LEAVE ME ALONE. I DON'T HAVE TIME TO MESS WITH YOU."

"Yes, sir. Thank you," I said.

I left, and again I returned the next day to greet him like I was seeing him for the first time.

"Hello, Mr. Butterball, I'm Les Brown."

"I know what your name is. Go get me some coffee. Make yourself useful."

I did just that. I set about making myself the most indispensable radio station errand boy in the history of broadcasting.

## Jockeying for a Position

You see, when you want something, you have to be willing to pay your dues. As the errand boy, I built trust. And I studied how the station worked. I became a human sponge, soaking up every spilled bit of information that had anything to do with that station.

I'd deliver food into the control room for the disc jockeys and then hang around watching them work, memorizing their hand movements on the control panel, until they'd ask me to leave. After a while, the disc jockeys came to like and

trust me. They even trusted me with their cars, sending me
to pick up entertainers arriving at the Miami International
Airport for interviews at the station.

I picked up Diana Ross and the Supremes, The Four
Tops, Sam Cook, The Temptations. I drove them all over
Miami Beach in the disc jockeys' big long Cadillacs. I didn't
have a driver's license, but I *acted* like I had one.

I was biding my time for some airtime. Then one day
my opportunity presented itself. One of the disc jockeys by
the name of Rock was drinking heavily while he was on the
air. It was a Saturday afternoon. *And there I was.* The only
one there.

I watched him through the control-room window. I
walked back and forth in front of that window, like a cat
watching the mouse. Saying, *"Drink, Rock. Drink!"*

I'd have gone and gotten him some more if he had asked
me. I was young. I was ready. And I was hungry.

Pretty soon, the phone rang. It was the station manager.
He said, "Les, this is Mr. Klein."

I said, "Yes, I know."

He said, "Rock can't finish his program."

I said, "Yes, sir, I know."

He said, "Would you call one of the other disc jockeys
to fill in?"

I said, "Yes, sir. I sure will, sir."

And when he hung the phone up, I said, "Now, he
must think I'm *crazy.*"

I called up my Mama and my girlfriend Cassandra, and
I told them "Ya'll go out on the front porch and turn up the
radio, I'M ABOUT TO COME ON THE AIR!"

I waited fifteen or twenty minutes and called the station
manager back. I said, "Mr. Klein, I can't find NOBODY!"

He said, "Young boy, do you know how to work the
controls?"

I said, "Yes, sir."

He said, "Go in there, but don't say anything. Hear me?"

I said, "Yes, sir."

I couldn't wait to get old Rock out of the way. I went in there. Took my seat behind that turntable. Flipped on the microphone and let 'er rip:

*Look out, this is me, L.B., triple P. Les Brown, your platter-playin' papa. There were none before me and there will be none after me, therefore that makes me the one and only. Young and single and love to mingle, certified, bona fide, indubitably qualified to bring you satisfaction, a whole lot of action. Look out, baby, I'm your LOVE man.*

*I WAS HUNGRY!*

[See exercises for this chapter in the Action Planner on page 236.]

# Three

## The Power to Change

*I know of no more encouraging fact than the unquestionable ability of man to elevate his life by conscious endeavor.*

—HENRY DAVID THOREAU

I will never forget the day the principal came into my fifth-grade classroom while we were clowning around, throwing paper, running, turning chairs over, acting wild. The teacher had left the room unattended and the class went crazy. Until the principal showed up.

She was outraged. Trouble had been brewing for several of us for some time. And it was at this moment that the principal made a decision that was to have a powerful impact on my life. In her anger, she began pointing at the most troublesome students and calling us names. "These students are stupid, dumb, retarded. They don't need to be here," she said. *"They need to be put back.*

"I want that one, that one and that one." She pointed at about six students. Including me. I remember the look on her face, the anger and the disgust her expression held. She was set on teaching us a lesson, on punishing us and making us pay. I remember the fear and hurt welling up inside me.

I said, "No, you are making a mistake! I'm not stupid!"

With that, they took us out of the fifth-grade class and put us back in the fourth grade as special-education students. I was kept in that category all through high school. It has taken me a long time to escape that label.

And in adulthood, much of my drive to succeed has been fueled by the devastating memory of that day in class when I was judged to be "slow" and without much promise. That memory has fueled my hunger to be somebody. It is a memory that still pricks at me, a memory that for a time shamed and stunted me but now drives me always to reaffirm my sense of who I am.

Later, the principal told my mother that they had put me back a grade for my own good. She said they were trying to help me. She was very courteous and persuasive. My mother, who had little formal schooling herself, went along. She felt she had no choice.

## The Dodo Ward

Most people do not realize how detrimental negative labels can be; they become self-fulfilling prophecies. I began to believe that I couldn't do certain things and if I encountered any classroom difficulty, I would stop.

Actually, there were few difficulties or demands once I was relegated to the "dodo ward," as other students called it. Not much was expected of us dodos. School became a breeze. I would laugh at the students who had to do algebra or trigonometry. I rarely even had homework assigned. The last laugh was on me, of course.

In my naïveté, I thought I was getting off easy, but in fact, I spent many years of my adulthood trying to catch up. I still have problems with some basic mathematics. I have a mental block about taking written tests. I probably am restricted or damaged in ways that I am not even aware of.

Hurtful memories can stifle your development and growth. How do we break through this insidious mental conditioning? How do we grow and develop beyond hurtful episodes that bury themselves in our subconscious and influence our lives? How do we change and grow so that we can live our dreams?

The first step is to break the hold of these inhibiting influences from the past. Recognize them and then either get rid of them or turn them into a positive force that pushes you ahead rather than holds you back.

Identify these inhibiting memories in your life so that you control *them* rather than allowing them to control *you*. Did someone hurt your feelings? Forgive them and forget it. Move on. Did someone punish you unfairly? It's over. It's done. Go on.

Here are a few of the most common emotions that burrow into the subconscious and impede our growth as individuals:

• *Anger.* This is a natural response to a perceived attack or injury. It makes energy flow. But when allowed to simmer, it depletes energy that could be used to improve your life. If you hold your anger for more than a week, it is only hurting you. Make yourself let go. Envision yourself throwing it out. Ease your mind. Transform your anger into positive motivation. Don't get mad, get motivated.

• *Revenge.* The first cousin of anger. It also robs you of strength in the long run. The person who has injured you has probably gone on with life; so should you. Don't let the injury hurt you further by inhibiting your growth. Lose it or use it. Instead of saying, "I'll get them," say, *"I'll show them. I'LL BE SOMEBODY!"*

• *Sadness.* This is more crippling than anger because it drains you from the start, sapping your will to go on. You probably will have to let this drain away slowly at its own pace. Time heals, but if the sadness seems to linger, consciously force it out. Seek out things that make you laugh and feel positive about life. Realize that feeling sad will not change anything. Seek peace of mind as your right.

• *Resentment.* Life is not always fair. It is unrealistic to feel any other way, and holding on to resentment is no way to fight back. Drop it and get back into the battle.

• *Guilt* is another emotion that stands between you and your dreams. All of us have done things we feel bad about and regret. Things we would do differently. Many of us carry that guilt around and it keeps us from moving forward. Don't let people put you on a guilt trip. Say to yourself when someone is putting you on the defensive, *"No matter what you do or say to me, I am still a worthwhile person."*

To rid yourself of these past emotions, put them in a perspective that is positive rather than negative and thereby cut off their painful roots in your subconscious. Reinterpret the past with these methods:

• *Get better, not bitter.* Find a quiet, comfortable place. Sit back and relax. Think about something or someone who caused you pain or disappointment. Now take a mental step back from that feeling and the situation. Assess it. Did the emotions that resulted make you stronger? Did they give you determination? Can you use those memories to empower you rather than drain you? Why let them hurt you further?

• *Envision those hurtful emotions as a sword held by an enemy.* In your mind, see yourself snatching the sword away and using it to cut away the emotional snares that have tied you up.

• *Get rid of regret.* If you are burdened by something you did, analyze it. Was it a business failure? Was it something foolish you said or did that hurt someone you care about? If so, apologize. That often clears the air, but use discretion if you think it might make matters worse. If you owe money to someone, pay them. Or tell them you intend to pay them a little at a time.

Whatever the cost, it is worth it to clear away burdensome emotions. If you have feelings of unworthiness because of something you did, let them go. Realize that we usually do the best we can according to our level of consciousness at the time. If you would not do the same thing again, you have changed. You are no longer the same person. That person is gone, so forgive yourself.

Love yourself unconditionally, just as you love those closest to you despite their faults. *Let it go so you can grow.* You have the power to change.

## *Mr. Washington to the Rescue*

After I was pulled out of class, put back a year and labeled mentally handicapped, my life did not find a path again until high school. A principal had knocked me off course, but a very special teacher, with a few liberating words, opened the possibilities of life to me again and gave me a larger vision for myself as a young man with a future.

Mr. LeRoy Washington, the school's celebrated speech and drama instructor, told me some things we all need to understand so that we may become masters of our own destiny. I was drawn to Mr. Washington because of his powerful presence and his reputation as a mentor for young people. Through sheer audacity, I crashed his classes and rehearsals without being officially enrolled or invited. I became a familiar, if not particularly welcome, presence. I hung around so much that one day, during a rehearsal in which I had no official part, Mr. Washington called upon me to write something on the blackboard for him.

I was bold in many ways, but I was not enthused about having to display my paltry aptitude for spelling and handwriting in front of Mr. Washington's elite.

"I . . . I . . . I can't do that, sir," I said.

"Why not?" he inquired.

Too embarrassed to remind Mr. Washington in front of his class that I was a special-education student, I told him only that I was a student in the class of the man whom everyone knew to be the special-education teacher.

"It doesn't *matter*," Mr. Washington stated. "GO to the board and follow my directions."

I was mortified.

"I can't do that, sir."

"WHY NOT?" he demanded.

"Because I am educable mentally retarded," I muttered.

Mr. Washington was a trained actor. He knew a dramatic moment when he was presented with one. He rose from his desk like King Neptune from the sea, fixed me in his gaze and delivered the lines that set my life on a new course.

"DO NOT EVER SAY THAT AGAIN!" he intoned. "Someone's opinion of you does NOT have to become YOUR reality."

On the one hand, I was humiliated for having acknowledged my supposed inferiority in front of Mr. Washington and his students. On the other, I felt the first tinglings of a liberation. *Someone expected things of me.*

Up to that point, I had been stuck. My life was on hold because I'd been given a label I was stuck with it. I did not think change was possible. I was going nowhere because that is exactly where I was expected to go. But from that moment, my life began to follow a new course.

## Getting Unstuck

The more I came to understand Mr. Washington's words the more clearly I saw the way ahead. Because this powerful figure, my teacher, saw through the label that had been affixed to me, I did too. I realized that someone else's opinion of me did not matter, what people thought of me was not important. What *was* important was how I perceived *myself*.

The limitations you have and the negative things that you internalize are given to you by the world. The things that empower you—the possibilities—*come from within*.

You must give yourself love and open yourself to the possibilities of life. Whatever your dream, know that it is *possible* to change your life and go after it. Marcus Aurelius said, "The universe is change; our life is what our thoughts make it."

Mr. Washington helped me get started, but you can get *yourself* unstuck. Here are a few things to try.

• *Work harder toward your goals*. Just the act of working harder focuses your mind and your actions, pulling you out of lethargy and into becoming an active life-force again.

• *Be creative and change your approach to life*. Get those wheels turning. Feel the energy flowing. Look for new ways to solve your problems.

• *Modify your goal*. Goals galore exist out there. Find one, get on top of it and climb to the next highest.

• *Ask for help*. Support groups work. They tell you that you are not alone, and they are run by people who often understand exactly where you are coming from and where you need to go.

• *Stay busy*. Don't make major decisions if you are depressed or frightened, but keep moving, feel your life-force in the motion. You have control.

• Listen to *positive* music, watch *positive* videos or movies, hang out with *positive*, upbeat people. The last thing a blue mood needs is more blues. Don't be a volunteer victim; be a fighter.

Sometimes I believe it is best to take the child's approach to life, which assumes no limitations at all. Children set out to do things without knowing that they are not *supposed* to be able to do them. And often, to our adult amazement and/or chagrin, they succeed anyway. *"How DID you climb out of that crib?"*

How do you climb out of your mental cellar? Just do it. Take action. Take charge of your emotions. Expect things to get better. Take the energy you are wasting feeling sorry for yourself and use it to help someone else. Accept responsibility for changing your life.

You can't expect to achieve new goals or move beyond your present circumstances unless YOU change. A friend of mine has a saying: *"If you want to continue getting what you are getting, just keep doing what you've been doing."* New avenues of achievement require a commitment to growth. The exploration of those avenues reveals talents that you never dreamed you possessed and opens you up to outlets for them that you never knew existed.

## Grow with the Flow: Change for the Good

Fred Luster was a steelworker until he was laid off. He wasted no time moaning and groaning and getting himself stuck. He'd always had a knack for cutting hair, so he became a barber. He found that he had a knack not just for barbering but for the entire field of personal grooming.

Fred, whose education was forged in steel mills rather than university classrooms, built Luster Products, a multimillion-dollar corporation. If Fred Luster can reinvent his life, if Mrs. Mamie Brown's boy can escape a background of poverty and educational pigeonholing, why shouldn't you be able to overcome any obstacles in your own path?

I have come to believe that many people react to adversity as I did to being labeled mentally retarded. Instead of seizing control and trying to change, they drop out of life. Somewhere along the line they were told they were not intelligent enough, athletic enough, attractive enough or lovable enough to aspire to greater things, so they gave up.

In spite of my upbringing in less than affluent surroundings, I did not feel poor or deprived and I was not afraid to dream of great things for myself. The stigma of being placed in a class for mentally retarded students knocked me off course for a while. But Mr. Washington put me back on track.

Once I absorbed the full meaning of Mr. Washington's words, I realized that the only important thing was my self-image. The same holds true for you. The only thing that can really stop you from living your dreams is *you*. Be willing to take charge of your life and change it for the better.

## Winners and Losers

I believe there are three kinds of people. There are winners, who know what they want and understand their potential and the possibilities. They take life on. Next are losers, who don't have a clue as to who they are. They allow circumstances to shape their lives and their self-image.

I believe there is a third group as well. This consists of potential winners whose lives are just slightly out of alignment. I call them wayward winners. It may be that they just need to learn how to be real winners. Perhaps they've hit a bump or two that has knocked them off course and they are temporarily befuddled. A failed relationship, a lost job, financial problems, unformed goals, a lack of parental support, illness—many things can send us off course temporarily.

Wayward winners are not lost souls; they just need some tweaking and coaching and nudging to get them back on course. A map might be nice. Many of these wayward winners are easily identifiable because they are *always searching*.

My persistence in shadowing Mr. Washington was an example of that. Although I certainly can't claim that I knew what I was doing, I believe now that I was instinctively searching for a way to get back on track.


## Believe in Yourself

Right now, there are many wayward winners out there braving rain, sleet and snow because they too still believe that they have untapped talents. They attend motivational seminars and listen to inspirational tapes and they plunge onward, believing that sooner or later they will find their way again.

Other wayward winners have temporarily given up. They are damaged and disoriented, their confidence badly eroded. They tend to drift through life numbly. Howard Thurman writes of these people in his book *Deep Is the Hunger*. He believes that they hunger for balance and direction in life. Deep down, their unconscious tells them, *"God, there's got to be more. This cannot be it for my life."* And they are right. There IS more.

The friends and relatives and loved ones of wayward winners see that they are out of sync and wonder why they can't be satisfied, why they don't settle down. They wonder how people who have such obvious abilities and great potential can be so disoriented and unsure.

It is difficult for others to understand the rawness of a broken heart or the aching emptiness of an unguided spirit. You and I know. We have been there. Wayward winners know that there are possibilities out there, but too often they feel locked out from them. Some are afraid to risk any more because of what they have risked and lost already. My fear of going to the blackboard for Mr. Washington was a risk avoidance. I was afraid of being knocked back farther.

I know now that as difficult as it may be for you wayward winners to do, it is necessary to continue to test yourselves. Even though you have been hurt before, it is the only way to grow. We all have the capacity to change, to lead meaningful and productive lives by awakening our consciousness.

I perceive consciousness as more than just awareness; I see it as a potential energy force comprised of your thoughts and feelings and impressions. I view consciousness as an active dimension of the human mind, not merely a passive vault where thoughts are stored.

Once activated, this consciousness becomes a driving life-force to be used for your betterment and the betterment of those around you. After all, if one highly motivated mind can make a difference, consider how much more a collective force can accomplish.

## Prepare for Liftoff

You know there are going to be tough times as you go about changing your life, so brace yourself and you will be able to handle them. When you get into your seat on an airplane, what is the first thing they tell you to do? Fasten your seat belt. Brace yourself for the turbulence.

When you decide to move your life to the next level of accomplishment, you must fasten your mental and spiritual seat belts because it is going to be a while before you reach that comfortable level again. You will reach it, but you must endure the turbulence of change in order to grow.

Try this technique to help you through the difficult times of change and growth. Find four reasons why you cannot succumb to your fears and your troubles. Find those deep sources of motivation that can lift you out of the turbulence and above the clouds.

You must change your life because, for example:

• You have not yet tapped the talents given you.
• You want to leave something more for your children.
• You want to live life rather than letting life live you.
• You want to do what makes YOU happy.

It is in these rocky early moments of bringing change to your life that you discover who you are. In the prosperous times, you build what is in your pocket. In the tough times, you strengthen *what is in your heart*. And that is when you gain insight into yourself, insight that leads to self-mastery and an expansion of your consciousness as a life-force in both your personal and professional lives.

How many times have you said that you wanted to do something and then talked yourself out of it? Fourteen years ago, I saw my first motivational speaker and I thought, "I could do that." I was inspired by Zig Zigler, who is one of the greatest and most successful in the field. I heard him and thought that I would like to do what he was doing.

During his speech, I leaned over to the guy next to me and asked how much Zigler was getting paid. The guy told me $5,000. And I said, "I KNOW I can do that!"

## Be Positively Charged

But it took nine years for me to act on that positive notion because the negatives flowed in behind it like sins chasing a saint. On the way home from that speech, my nagging inner conversations started in, *"Les Brown, you can't do that. You don't have a college education. You've never worked for a major corporation. What makes you think you can earn more in one hour talking than you've made working a whole month?"*

On that trip home, my dream got shoved into the back-seat and beaten up. Life is an ongoing war with insecurities and fears. I won a major battle when Mr. Washington came to my aid in high school, but there are always new battles to fight. In this case, I allowed the negative and self-defeating image of myself, that lower consciousness, to dominate my thinking. I dwelt upon the circumstances of my past and present instead of trusting in my *abilities* and focusing on the *possibilities*.

When you have such negative inner conversations telling you that you don't have the time or the money or the training or the contacts or you are not good enough, do this: *Ignore them* and take action to change your situation. People who are deterred by negative inner conversations are like the first frog that fell into a bottle of milk. This frog cursed his luck, hopped around in anger, gave up and died.

Those who take the positive approach and fight for their dreams are like the second frog that fell in. This one cursed his luck, but kept on kicking. He directed his anger toward positive action. This highly focused frog kicked until he churned that milk into butter, and then he hopped out.

You have to disregard all those other voices and listen to your own. Years ago there was a belief that the world was flat. People were born into that belief and they took it on faith that if they went too far from the shoreline in a boat they would fall off the earth. Columbus just sailed on.

Be like Christopher Columbus. Disregard the know-it-alls and set sail. In more modern times, test pilot Chuck Yeager, the guy with the "Right Stuff," was told by some of aviation's best scientists that if he became the first man to break the sound barrier he could burn up. He might rattle apart in mid-air. Yeager believed in himself. He broke the sound barrier and lived to become an aviation pioneer and national folk hero. Believe in yourself. Know that you have the Right Stuff too.

All of our lives we have been told what we could not do, and too often we take that as fact. But people with limited visions of themselves can not possibly have a larger vision of you. The world is not flat and you CAN break through barriers to live your dreams.

## Never Too Old to Be Bold

And please note this: You are never too old to set another goal or to dream a new dream. A gentleman nearing retirement age once approached me after I'd given a speech to his corporation. He said, "You know, that was real great motivation for the young guys, but I've done all my work. There is nothing else for me to do."

I replied, "Oh yes, you have a lot to give. The fact that you are still here on this planet means that your business is NOT DONE."

A woman I have a great deal of respect for, the Reverend Johnnie Colemon of Christ Universal Temple in Chicago, was at an age where most people are sitting in a rocking chair when she set about building what is now one of the largest religious complexes in Chicago, seating 4,000 people. She also built her own restaurant and grade school also to serve her congregation. She did this although many of her advisers and bankers told her it was an impossible goal. She went right ahead and built a multimillion-dollar complex despite some very imposing challenges and circumstances—and she is still expanding it.

Few people realize it, but the late Sam Walton, the son of a small-town Oklahoma banker, was forty-five years old before he opened his first Wal-Mart store. Now that is not very old, but then, within the next few years, Sam went from being a well-to-do businessman to becoming one of the wealthiest and most successful men in the world.

Up to that point, he and a brother had put together a chain of fifteen Ben Franklin franchises after buying their first five-and-dime with a $25,000 loan in 1945. When the top executives at Ben Franklin refused to go along with Walton's idea of building bigger stores with smaller profit margins in small towns around the country, he set off on his own.

Most businessmen of that age would have played it safe. Sam Walton followed his own dream and became the most successful merchant of his time and the nation's wealthiest man. When he died at age seventy-four in April of 1992, his company had 1,735 stores in the United States and Mexico. His family fortune was estimated to be in excess of $23 billion.

He changed his life and followed his dream. And he achieved it. *He used life up.*

There are people who are wise enough and motivated enough to change their lives and live their dreams, and then there are those who need a kick in the pants to change their ways. I had a friend who belonged to the latter group.

## Change by Court Order

My friend Ronnie was a singer in Columbus while I was working there. I had promoted a few shows for him and I didn't know much about his personal life. He told me that he traveled a lot and that he had gotten into legal problems for not living up to the terms of a divorce settlement. I didn't know the details of his problems when he asked me to be a character witness at a court hearing; otherwise I probably would not have consented to testify on his behalf. I knew only that he definitely WAS a character.

I discovered during the court hearing that Ronnie was in court because he had neglected to keep up on his financial responsibilities toward his ex-wife and their four children. Ronnie's former wife brought all four of their children into court and they lined up against Ronnie, me and two members of his band who had also agreed to be character witnesses without really understanding what the hearing was about. I didn't agree with the way Ronnie had neglected his responsibility to his children. I hadn't known about his irresponsibility when I consented to testify.

As the hearing progressed, I became more and more uncomfortable with the situation. Just the presence of his children in the courtroom was almost enough to make me and the other character witnesses take a hike. Those four little ones looked as though Ronnie had spit them out. They were definitely HIS children.

During the hearing, his former wife put it out there beautifully. She told of the hardship of raising the children without a father and without financial support. She listed all the things that their children had to do without because of Ronnie's irresponsibility. His former wife was more than patient. She had warned him many times that she would take him to court if he did not pay child support as ordered in their divorce. He didn't listen and she finally had taken action.

She told her story with such grace and passion that by the time she completed her testimony, there was not a dry eye in the house—my eyes included. Ronnie's former wife had really won the sympathy of the entire courtroom. After hearing her testimony, the judge turned to Ronnie in exasperation.

"What do you have to say for yourself?" the judge asked him.

Ronnie didn't know what to say. He knew his goose was cooked. He knew he was dead wrong. He was so defeated, he just hung his head and said something silly.

"Oh, Your Honor, those kids don't even look like me."

But this judge was not in a silly mood.

"Well then, sir," he said angrily, "FEED THEM UNTIL THEY DO!"

The courtroom went wild with laughter. And when it did, I sneaked out. So did the other character witnesses. We didn't say a word on Ronnie's behalf. If he wasn't smart enough to change his life, we weren't going to hang around and watch him hang himself.

Get motivated and change your life before all your friends decide the same about you. Take charge of your life.

[See exercises for this chapter in the Action Planner on page 239.]

# Four

## Wake Up and Work on Your Dreams

*What do I mean by loving ourselves properly? I mean first of all, desiring to live, accepting life as a very great gift and a great good, not because of what it gives us, but because of what it enables us to give others.*

—THOMAS MERTON

When I lived in Columbus, Ohio, I drove twenty miles to work every day. There were mornings when I would get out of my car, put the key in the office door and suddenly think: *"How did I get here?"*

I had driven unconsciously, not thinking of what I was doing or where I was going. I was lost in the routine of the drive, in the familiarity of the scenery, in the comfort of my car.

Have you had the same sort of experience? I know a lot of folks who do things unthinkingly because they are locked into a habit or a behavior pattern. They cruise unconsciously through life, numb and unknowing. And when they come to the end of life still numb and unknowing, most of them probably wonder how they got there.

## This Is a Wake-up Call

You must *consciously* engage yourself in life in order to live your dreams. Aristotle said, "To be conscious of what we are perceiving or thinking is to be conscious of our own existence." A lot of people believe that they are doing all they are capable of doing with their lives. They don't see themselves as having anything vital or powerful within them. They cruise along based on their past experiences and limited awareness. People who live like this go to their graves with their greatness unrealized. Their talents and gifts will never be put to use.

## Four Stages of Greatness

In order to change so that you can live your dreams, you must grow in consciousness. This process of personal growth involves four stages of increased awareness in the areas of: *self-knowledge*, *self-approval*, *self-commitment* and *self-fulfillment*.

If you want to get a larger vision of yourself—that is, to acquire the ability to see yourself beyond your circumstances and mental conditioning—ask yourself, "What drives me?" Try to understand what influences are acting upon you. Many of us suffer from what I call "unconscious incompetence": We don't know what we don't know. So, in the beginning, you need to master *self-knowledge*. Before you can fully wake up and change your life, you must understand the frame of reference from which you see the world. "Know thyself" is an age-old maxim, but how well do you really know yourself? Who are you?

Lauren, an attractive, intelligent and dynamic person, was plagued by personal demons. She was generally quite pleasant and personable, but her friends and co-workers were wary of her hair-trigger temper. The slightest teasing would set her off. Anything short of praise was perceived as an attack.

Though successful in her work, she was highly insecure, and in her drive to climb up the ladder of her profession, she had obtained a reputation for being ruthless. She was aware of all these personality problems, yet she was unable to get a handle on them. And then a friend of hers confided that he had joined a support group for the grown children of alcoholics.

The friend described the inner torment that he had experienced and the personality problems that could be traced to his childhood conflicts with his father's alcoholism. The friend said that these problems related to a chronic lack of self-esteem that is typical of people who had grown up with an alcoholic parent.

Lauren wept with sadness but also in relief after talking with the friend, for she too was the child of an alcoholic parent and the psychological problems he had described were very similar to her own. She joined the support group, and over the course of several months, it changed her life and her outlook dramatically. Eventually, inner peace began to replace inner turmoil.

## Self-knowledge Sets You Free

Lauren thought she knew herself but she reached a new level of self-knowledge and a heightened consciousness when she began attending the support group. She learned how her experiences as the child of an alcoholic parent were affecting her development as an adult, and with that more complete self-knowledge, she was able to grow.

It troubles me that we spend years in school learning about the lives of other people, but we devote hardly any time at all to studying ourselves. Too many of us understand the forces of American or European history but not the forces behind our personal histories. A sense of self-knowledge grows out of contemplation and reflection, of questioning yourself and welcoming feedback from others. By knowing yourself, by consciously striving to understand how your personality was formed, you can free yourself to grow beyond your past experiences. You can live for the grand possibilities of the future, rather than be tied to the restrictive influences of the past.

I met the great actress Cicely Tyson recently and she and I were talking with a friend who aspires to be an actress. My friend Sheila is preparing for a role in which she must play an elderly woman and she is having difficulty with the characterization. She asked Cicely how she transformed herself for the role of Miss Jane Pittman. Cicely said that she never talked to elderly women or studied their actions for the role because each is different and there are no universal characteristics. Instead, she said, "I went within myself and BECAME old. You can go from acting coach to acting coach, but to get the essence of acting, you have to *know yourself first*. You must be able to go within and bring yourself out."

I once heard it said that everyone is born unique but most of us die copies. Learn who you are and work on bringing your true self out. Reflect on who you are and how you relate to the world. Look carefully at your past and you will come to a fuller understanding of who you presently are. You can do this by honestly examining the events, people and circumstances that have shaped you.

When you know yourself and understand your motivations, you become more aware of the tools that you possess—your unique mix of talents and abilities—and also the limitations you have. Understand that most of your limitations are self-imposed because of your history and that *your field of vision is too often limited by your experience instead of being guided by your imagination.*

## Change, Change, Change

Sometimes we have to discard the tools that we have long depended on and look to new ones. This is especially true in businesses where changing technology demands workers have the ability to change with it. Change is difficult but often essential to survival. At times in your life, you will have to change your approach just as Sam Walton did. At a time when many giant retail firms were struggling, Walton changed with the times and prospered.

The *Harvard Business Review* credited him with transforming the traditional approach to retailing. The standard procedure in the industry was for senior executives in corporate offices far from the aisles and shelves of their stores to make inventory purchasing and stocking decisions. Walton championed a new system in which individual store managers made those decisions, allowing the customers to pull products into the store rather than having corporate chiefs push goods at them. The results were spectacular sales and growth for his Wal-Mart and Sam's Wholesale Club retail empire.

When you grow in consciousness of the changing world around you, you begin to get a larger vision of yourself. As you gain self-knowledge you will see yourself differently and others will too. You will realize that you have abilities and talents and tools that you have not even begun to reach for. I jokingly tell my audiences that once you begin to really know yourself and know the truth of who you are, you will not even need an alarm clock anymore. You will wake up in the morning eager for the brand-new day. You will start walking 25 percent faster. You will be excited about YOU.

About your unfolding future. Instead of being *in* the way, you will be *on* your way.

To assist your growth in self-knowledge, try these steps. Write down the results and review them at least once a year so that you can begin to measure your progress at different points in your life.

- *Get to know what other people like about you*. Ask someone close to you to tell you honestly how he or she views you. Have that person rate you and your specific traits on a scale of one to five. Do people describe you as your own worst enemy? If they do, you need to work on your self-knowledge to understand why.
- *Determine what you expect to achieve in life*. This is what you *expect*, not what you hope or dream for.
- *Consider your life for a moment*. What drives you? What inhibits you?
- *Evaluate how you handle compliments*. This is a good barometer of how you feel about yourself because if you accept them naturally without seeking them out you have strong self-approval and a sense of worthiness. Can you accept compliments without discomfort, or do you always have to take exception or deflect them? Do you crave compliments to the point that you will do anything to get them?

## Self-approval

Once you begin to know and understand yourself more completely, then you must accept and love yourself. *Self-approval* is crucial to changing your life and pursuing your dreams and goals.

As Lauren discovered, the children of alcoholic parents often carry enormous guilt and insecurity because they blame themselves for their parent's drinking. Because of the restricted vision of children, they cannot understand that other influences cause the parent to drink. Children often think the alcoholic parent drinks because of *them*. This results in the child growing into adulthood with a very poor self-image.

I have seen children take on incredible burdens because of their limited vision of the world. I know of a girl whose brother died when she was in her early teens. The older brother was her hero. He was a straight-A student, a class leader, a popular guy. He died with no warning, no previous illness. He collapsed and died because of a blood clot in his brain. The girl was devastated, and in her limited vision, she blamed herself for his death. She took on enormous guilt because he died and she lived on. She once said that she should have died instead because she was not as good and smart as her brother. She carried a great weight into adulthood, one that affected her relationships and her ability to fully engage her gifts and talents.

Self-hatred, guilt and long-standing anger block your growth. Practice self-love and forgiveness and they will carry over into your relationships, your work and the world around you. By loving yourself, you open up the possibility for others to love you, too. Work to remove the psychological blinders that restrict your own growth. Understand yourself and your motives and the influences in your life and open yourself up. Direct your energy away from self-destruction or self-loathing. Forgive yourself. Forgive those who have hurt you. Give yourself self-approval and permission to move on.

Right now, write down all your bad habits and faults and all the mistakes you have made in your life. Did you hurt someone? Did you malign someone? Did you waste an opportunity?

Have you written down everything that has nagged and eaten at you over the years? Good. Now take that piece of paper, tear it to shreds and throw it away. Forgive yourself for your faults and your mistakes and move on. The way to your dreams is now clear!

Each of us has a basic goodness that is the foundation for what we can ultimately achieve. Look for that goodness within yourself. Try these steps if you need to boost your self-approval.

• Consider your gifts. *I am a good communicator. I have good health. I am loved by my family and friends.*
• Write down at least five things that you like about yourself. *I am mindful of my appearance. I am punctual. I am honest. I am loving. I am concerned about others.*
• Call to mind the people who make you feel special. What do these people inspire in you?
• Recall moments of triumph when you did well at work or in school. Capture that feeling of self-satisfaction again.

## An Uncommon Life

Life is more meaningful when you are always looking to grow and working toward a goal. Seek self-approval by making yours an uncommon life that you can be proud of. Former President Theodore Roosevelt possessed vast amounts of self-approval. Here is his philosophy:

> *I choose not to be a common man. Me, it's my right to be uncommon if I can. I'll seek opportunity, not security. I do not wish to be a kept citizen—humbled and dulled by having the state look after me. I want to take the calculated risk, to dream and to build, to fail and to succeed. I'll refuse to live from hand to mouth. I'll prefer the challenges of life to the guaranteed existence. The thrill of fulfillment to the stale calm of Utopia. I will never cower before any master nor bend to any friend. It is my heritage to stand erect, proud and unafraid, to think and act for myself and face the world boldly and say, "This I have done."*

What an uncommon person! Of course, being uncommon means you may be criticized. Be prepared for that. Be prepared for people to block you and conspire against you. Even your own family may challenge your ability to choose your own way. You can't always expect those close to you to see your dream. I know of a fellow named Larry, whose mother and father wanted him to follow the family tradition and become a doctor. So he went to medical school and was doing very well. Then he started hearing an inner voice that had something else in mind for him. Larry loved making people laugh. He had a dream of doing that. Often, if you don't listen to an inner voice and summon the courage to live your dream, life will make you so miserable you will HAVE to do it. Larry became miserable. He decided that he had to get out of medical school. So he told his parents.

Think about his position here. Larry loved and respected his parents. He faced the people whom he most wanted to believe in him—*people who had paid tens of thousands in tuition for him*. He courageously said, "Mom and Dad, I have dropped out of medical school to pursue my dream."

They said, "Well, son, what is your dream?"

And he replied, *"I want to become a clown."*

"Don't make jokes, son, this is serious. What is it you really want to do?"

"I want to become a clown and make people laugh."

"I'll tell you how to make people laugh," his father said. "Go to the hospital and tell them that you have dropped out of medical school to become a clown! They'll crack up and then they'll call the people with the white jackets!"

Well, Larry pursued his dream anyway. He went to Los Angeles, got on television and became so well known that he couldn't meet the demand for his act. He ended up hiring other clowns and starting a clown service that made over $400,000 in its first year! That's nothing to laugh at.

As Henry David Thoreau said, "If a man does not keep pace with his companions, perhaps it is because he hears a different drummer. Let him step to the music which he hears, however measured or far away."

Once you have expanded your self-knowledge and learned self-approval, the next step is *self-commitment*.

If you want to change your life, commit yourself to doing it and don't expect everyone else to fall in behind you. Do something that advances your life every day, however small a step it might be. *Begin to read a book that will help you move toward your dream. Write a letter to an expert seeking advice. Mail a résumé.*

The evangelist Dr. Robert Schuller began his ministry in an abandoned drive-in theater and built it into a church with tens of thousands of members who worship in the architectural wonder that he built, the Crystal Cathedral. His philosophy is *"By the yard, it's hard. But inch by inch, anything is a cinch."*

## Self-commitment

When you decide to take life on, it opens up for you. You become aware of things that you were not aware of before. It's similar to the expanded consciousness that comes whenever I commit to a diet. Suddenly everywhere I look there is *FOOD*! The same sort of thing occurs when you buy a new car. Suddenly, you notice cars exactly like it everywhere you go. Right? Your consciousness of those similar cars has been expanded because you bought one. When you make a commitment, when your life awareness is expanded, when your consciousness is tuned, opportunities previously unseen begin to appear. If you view all the things that happen to you, both good and bad, as *opportunities*, then you operate out of a higher level of consciousness. In this posture, you are running your life, rather than running *from* life.

What is it that, in the past, you thought about but decided you could not do? What have you talked yourself out of? Whatever it was, bring it back. Commit to it. How are you going to do it? That will come to you in due time. You see, you don't get in life what you want. *You get in life what you are.* And the good news is that you can always get more in life by working to develop yourself.

Here are a few examples for taking charge of your life through self-commitment:

• If you have a weight problem, go into a bakery, smell those pastries, inhale deeply, and then walk out. One small step toward self-commitment, one giant step away from massive calorie counts.

• If you have difficulty making decisions, make small ones for practice. Decide to paint the living room. Decide to put shelves up in the garage. Do it.

• Do something that makes you anxious. Do your taxes. Call your in-laws. Ask the boss to lunch.

• Write down two things that you will do this week just to make yourself stronger. *I will lose two pounds. I will ride my bicycle continuously for an hour.* Commit yourself to doing them.

• List at least three actions you will commit yourself to taking. One short-term or within a month: *I will have my résumé put together.* One mid-term, within six months: *I will have interviewed with at least three employers.* One long-term, within five years: *I will be working for another company in a more responsible position and earning twice my current income.* Write them all down, otherwise these are merely wishes.

Once you accept yourself as a person worthy of your goals, commitment flows naturally. No one who feels greatness within must be forced out of bed in the morning. You need a channel for your commitment and a framework from which to manage it as far as time, resources, emotions and relationships. You need to make a commitment, and once you make it, then life will give you some answers.

## Make the Leap

You cannot just sit on the side of the pool and stick your toe in. You have got to be willing to make the leap. Now, most people do not want to do that. They want to perch on the side and say, "Tell me, is it cold in there? Is it rough in there?" Well, forget your fears and your self-concern, dive in and see. The German philosopher and writer Johann Wolfgang von Goethe said:

> Until one is committed, there is hesitance, the chance to draw back. Always ineffectiveness. Concerning all acts of initiative (and creation), there is one elemental truth the ignorance of which kills countless ideas and splendid plans; that the moment one commits oneself, then providence moves too. All sorts of things occur to help one that would never have otherwise occurred. A whole stream of events issues from the decision, raising in one's favor all manner of unforeseen incidents and meetings and material assistance which no man could have dreamed would come his way. Whatever you can do or dream you can begin it. Boldness has genius, power and magic in it. Begin it now.

## Commitment Leads to Self-fulfillment

Once you have committed to something and achieved it, you experience self-fulfillment—the feeling of success and empowerment. I believe we should consider the drive for self-fulfillment to be an unending quest. Your life should be a continuous cycle of testing self-knowledge, fortifying self-approval, renewing self-commitment and striving for new levels of *self-fulfillment*.

It is fine to acknowledge your accomplishments and savor your victories, but there is not enough time in life to rest on your laurels for long. Justice Oliver Wendell Holmes said,

"The work never is done while the power to work remains. . . . For to live is to function. That is all there is in living."

I believe you should never stop setting new goals. When you reach a goal and feel fulfilled, celebrate your accomplishment, tell yourself you earned it, but remember that what is important is *who you are*, not what you have done or what you are going to do. Character and principle are the true measures of your value. Justice Holmes also said, "What lies behind us and what lies before us are tiny matters compared to what lies within us."

All of us need to grow continuously in our lives. If you are the same person now that you were a year ago or even a day ago, then you are not growing. In order to move toward greatness, you must consciously endeavor to expand and free yourself from your own limitations—from your past, from your fears and from the crippling opinions of others.

The only real obstacle in your path to a fulfilling life is you, and that can be a considerable obstacle because you carry the baggage of insecurities and past experience. But by using the four-stage cycle of personal growth, you can overcome such obstacles and pursue your dreams. Once you have accomplished a goal and reached a level of self-fulfillment, then it is time to go back to the first stage in the cycle so that you can continue to grow.

• *Review your self-knowledge.* Has accomplishing your goal changed you? For the better or for the worse? How do friends perceive you now? What have you learned? How can you apply it?

• *Reexamine your level of self-approval.* Are you more comfortable with yourself because of this latest accomplishment or are you less at ease? Why?

• *Renew your commitment to personal growth.* Charge up. Set your sights on something new that will contribute to the betterment not only of yourself but of the world around you.

• Set a course for a new level of self-fulfillment.

## Charge Up and Change Your Life

To stay in the cycle of continuous growth, you have got to have deep reservoirs of energy. If you are excited about what you do, whether it is selling cars, making speeches or building bridges, people will come to watch your energy burn.

Bob Boyde, a friend of mine, sold soap. And Bob has extremely deep reservoirs of energy. I had plenty of soap when he came to me, but Bob soft-soaped me. He rubbed soap in my eyes. He washed my mouth out with soap. He buried me in soap bubbles.

He was so enthusiastic about his product that I bought $3,000 worth of soap. It was in my bathroom, my living room, my dining room. My former wife thought I had gone completely insane! But I bought into Bob's dream because he believed so *strongly* in it. He was deeply committed.

I had to. You see, I had helped Bob work on his commitment, and I got him so committed that even I couldn't resist. Bob came to me another time. I don't know how he got past the stacks of soap boxes, but he did. He said, "Les, I've got this idea. Man, we are going to make a whole lot of money."

That is what I admire about Bob. Even though Bob has had his share of failed ventures in the past, he has never lost any of his fire. Bob epitomizes the attitude that Sir Winston Churchill referred to when he said, "Courage is the capacity to go from failure to failure without losing enthusiasm."

You must be courageous in pursuing your dreams. And, like Bob, ENTHUSIASTIC.

Bob said, "Les, man, I've been working on this idea. You, with all the exposure you've got, man, you could make a fortune with this. This thing is a MONEY MACHINE."

He got to me, as always.

Bob was so excited about his dream that I bought into it. People are attracted by excitement and enthusiasm. They don't want to be around the living dead. Let the dead bury the dead. Keep the dead away from you.

Be excited about whatever it is that you do. Be contagious. People are looking at you and they want to know if you truly believe in your vision.

If you are not positive, if you are not energetic, if you are not excited about your OWN dream, how can you expect anybody else to be?

Tell yourself: *"I'm going to be fired up about my dreams! I'm going to do it with everything I've got!"*

A lot of people try once or twice, and if they meet with defeat, they use those experiences as an excuse to give up. Bob knows himself. He likes himself. He is committed. And no matter how many failures or successes he has, he is always seeking new levels of self-fulfillment.

Bob and I are both fans of a saying by M. H. Alderson that goes: "If at first you don't succeed, you are running about average."

You failed?

SO WHAT?

You made the average.

Know that you can beat it and better it.

[See exercises for this chapter in the Action Planner on page 243.]

# Five

## Live Your Dreams

*It must be borne in mind that the tragedy of life does not lie in not reaching your goals, the tragedy lies in not having any goals to reach. It isn't a calamity to die with dreams unfulfilled, but it is a calamity not to dream. It is not a disaster to be unable to capture your ideals, but it is a disaster to have no ideals to capture. It is not a disgrace not to reach the stars, but it is a disgrace to have no stars to reach.*

—Dr. Benjamin Isaiah Mays

*If you don't dream you might as well be dead.*

—George Foreman

The winos frequented the corner of Tenth and Fourth in Overtown because there was a beer and wine store there. When I walked past them I was always wary. I could see the deadness in their eyes. One or two would be sprawled on the ground, reeking of urine and alcohol and life gone to rot.

A few of my schoolmates would play hooky and they'd hang out with those winos, begging them for hits off the bottles in their brown bags. A voice inside kept me away from those lifeless men and their life-draining bottles. "That is not going to be your destiny," it said. It was a powerful voice. It had to be.

Something within me seemed certain that my destiny lay elsewhere even though I had seen a frightful number of my neighbors aspire to better lives and fall short. I'd seen some go off to college and seem to be well on their way to escaping the corner of Tenth and Fourth, only to be drawn back because they were not prepared or equipped to succeed. They had gotten out of Overtown, but they had not gotten Overtown out of them.

In Overtown, people lived either in apartments that we compared to doghouses because they had no back doors, or in what were called "shotgun houses." The rooms were more or less in a line from front to back so that if a shotgun was fired at the front, the pellets would go straight through the house.

Today Overtown is known for crippling poverty. It was not such a bad place then, but there were areas that you did not wander into if you valued your money and your safety. The worst section was an area known as "Bucket of Blood." Its conditions were adequately described by that name, and by the signs in the emergency room of nearby Jackson Memorial Hospital that said, DO YOUR CUTTING AND SHOOTING ON MONDAY AND TUESDAY. AVOID THE WEEKEND RUSH.

I knew physical escape from my neighborhood was possible because people I'd known had moved into nice houses in more affluent areas. My mother introduced me to a teacher, a man whom people often said I resembled. He had a smile like mine, they said. Empowered by that kinship, I visited his home once with my mother. It seemed palatial to my eyes. The carpet was a marvel to my linoleum-trained feet.

I remember my mother saying that she had known this man when he was a child of my age, and that he had gone from high school to college and graduated and done well in life.

She held him up for me to admire and model myself after. And I did that. I looked at his big, beautiful house, and I remember telling myself, "This is *possible* for me."

## Identify Your Dream and Know That
## It Is Possible

My mother is a wise woman. It was not within her means to take her family out of Overtown and into such homes as this man had acquired. But she worked hard to expose us to the possibilities in life. She planted seeds of purpose and ambition.

Those seeds took root. Once I grasped the possibility of a life beyond Overtown and its smothering environment, I began to expect great things for myself.

Truth be told, I put myself in a grand house long before I had any rightful claim. One night, after a high-school play, I was offered a ride home by some of my much wealthier classmates from Miami Beach. Embarrassed to have them see the shotgun house I belonged to in Overtown, I had them drop me off in front off a doctor's mansion miles from my home, one that I had often admired.

My friends who had given me a ride were impressed with the house. So impressed, they wanted to come in with me and look around. They wanted to swim in the pool. *No*, I said. *Not tonight*. They refused to drive away. They hung around, making noise. *I* wanted to get out of there before the police came around. I had hoped to wave good-bye, see them disappear in the distance and catch a bus.

I was a great deal less affluent than the standard resident of this neighborhood. I was so broke back then, if I just *walked* by a bank, the alarms went off. To get rid of my friends, I began walking toward the front door of the house, "Ya'll take it easy," I said. "Good night. See ya!"

To my dismay, they had very fine manners.

"We'll wait until you get inside and blink the light," they offered.

"Oh, no," I insisted, "This is a heavily protected area and someone might call the police if you wait around too long. Ya'll better go now. I'll be fine. Besides, I have to go around back because the key is hidden back there."

Finally, they drove off. I walked slowly toward the door to make sure they didn't circle, and then I ran like a crazy man to the bus station.

The next day I was the talk of the cast. *"That Les Brown, what a mansion he's living in,"* they said. Not yet, I thought back then. *But it's possible.*

## Pursue the Dream

To have dreams is the first step toward making them realities. Once you have squared yourself with your past, approved of yourself, and committed to seeking self-fulfillment, next allow yourself to dream. Chart your course. Envision yourself achieving those dreams.

Once you have dared to dream, I believe you MUST pursue that dream. If you do not pursue your dreams they will consume you; the knowledge that you had a dream but did not pursue it is killing knowledge. Consider it absolutely necessary to go after your dreams. José Ortega y Gasset said, "Human life, by its very nature, has to be dedicated to something."

Without goals in your professional, personal and spiritual life, you are just looking. You are not actively engaged in this world. Not having goals is like having no idea where you want to go when you step up to an airline counter to buy a ticket. You lug your baggage up. Life says, "Where will you be flying to today?" And you reply, "Gee, I don't know." Without *direction*, without *goals*, you can't BUY a ticket in this life.

## Make This Your Decade

In order to make this your decade, you have to set *specific goals* and you have to be strongly motivated to reach them. Put your goals down on paper. It makes them more real to you. It gives your goals and thoughts weight and permanence.

Write down your five greatest dreams.

1. I want to buy my mother a grand house where she can entertain her friends and sit on the porch and warm herself in the sun.
2. I want to be a nationally known public speaker with a message that will better the world.
3. I want to write a whole series of books that will inspire people in the same way.
4. I want to have my own television show to reach an even greater audience than I can reach in person.
5. I want my children and grandchildren to be able to handle the challenges of life.

## Follow Your Dream

When I started working on my goal to become a professional public speaker five years ago, I had no training in a multibillion-dollar industry. I was not a celebrity with some instant entrée to the club. Neither athlete nor actor, I had no proven value in this vast market. I was an ant knocking on the door to the giant's castle.

I knew virtually nothing about the business. I did know, however, that I loved talking to people. I took pleasure in making them feel good and contributing to their understanding of themselves. Other than that, the only thing I had going for me was my enthusiasm for the work. I wanted to do something that would give my life value and meaning.

On my way to the front door of that dream, I'd lost all my money, I'd lost my car, I'd lost the place I lived, I had NOTHING. Nothing except the certainty that this is what I wanted to do with my life and the sense that it was possible.

As much as you may believe you have selected your goal, I believe your goal selects you. The universe uses you to its purpose. So allow it to happen. Give yourself to your dream and follow it wherever it takes you in glorious pursuit. For a while it may beat you up; hang on over the bumps and rough spots; enjoy the trip.

There will be times when you will feel alone and deserted, when you will feel weak and doubt yourself and wonder if you are stark raving mad, but if you endure and persevere, eventually you will arrive at your dream. The things you want are always possible; it is just that the way to get them is not always *apparent*. Once you decide to go after them, the way becomes clear.

I started on the way to my goal at the library, which is still the cheapest and best source of information in the world. I found books on public speaking and began reading all I could on the topic. I found a list of organizations for public speakers. I joined as many as I could. I studied the best speakers—their posture, their hand gestures, their inflections and their messages.

I talked with public speakers about their work. I asked them their secrets. They said practice was essential. So I volunteered to speak to schoolchildren because I knew they wouldn't be critical of my technique. I just needed the practice.

I spoke to grade-school students and then high-school students, and then all sorts of clubs and organizations. I spoke to any group that would listen and even many that didn't. I worked on my dream and I never let up. I may have wanted to. I may have been sorely tempted. But I hung on.

Even *I* would not have dared to predict five years ago, when I didn't have a car, a place to live or $10,000 to my name, that I would receive the highest award given by the

National Speakers Association or that the 170,000 members of Toastmasters International would select me as one of the world's best public speakers in 1991.

## Goals Get You Going

Goals give you a purpose for taking life on. People who live without goals have no purpose and it is obvious even in their body language. They are on permanent idle, they slouch, they list from side to side. Their conversations dawdle. They telephone you: "Hey, I'm just calling. I wasn't doing anything, so I thought I'd call you." *Well, don't call* ME. I'VE *got things to do.*

Many people just muddle through life. They don't read informational material, they don't even pay attention when they WATCH television. If you ask them what they are watching, they mumblemouth, *"Nothin', I'm just lookin'."*

What are your goals for your career? For your relationships? For your spiritual life? Develop a schedule for the next month, the next six months, the next year, five years and ten years. Write it all out.

Let's take one of the most common goals: You want to make more *money*. If that is your goal, then take some practical steps toward realizing it.

• First, determine specifically *how much* money you want to make. Then, double that amount and make THAT your goal. Even if you don't reach the higher amount, you will probably still find yourself making more than your original goal.

• Second, decide the *amount of energy you are willing to expend* to reach your goal. How many hours are you willing to work a day? How many jobs are you willing to hold down? What sort of work are you willing to do?

• A third step in this process is to *develop a practical plan of action and get started immediately.* Chart out where you want to be in relation to your goal in the next month, six months, one year, five years and ten years. Get started today. Go apply for that second job NOW! Go enroll in that career training program NOW! Ask for that raise NOW!

• And finally, make sure that you have all of this *written down* so that you can review it every morning and every night and envision yourself taking these steps, DOING THEM and SUCCEEDING!

## Road Maps to Success

Your goals are the road maps that guide you and show you what is possible for your life. Life takes on meaning when you become motivated, set goals and charge after them in an unstoppable manner. Goals help you channel your energy into action. They place you in charge of your life.

One of my goals as a young man was to buy my adoptive mother a house. As a boy, I told my Mama that I was going to buy her a house so that she would never have to work, and she could just stay home and fix me sweet-potato pies. (My Mama fixes sweet-potato pies that you can't eat with your shoes on: You have to take your shoes off so you can wiggle your toes!)

Another goal of mine was to see that my children had a better life than mine. You need deep purposes like that; they drive you. I *know* my goals have served me in challenging times. Those two goals have had a *definite* impact on my life.

Once, when I was competing for a contract with a large company, I sat at a table facing two men representing my competition. They sized me up. I overheard one tell the other, "This guy doesn't have any credentials. We have the advantage. We've got TWO Ph.D.s between us."

Upon hearing that, I got up from the table and went to the rest room. I took myself for a motivational walk. I said to myself, *"Les Brown, what do you care about their two Ph.D.s? You have SIX CHILDREN and a MAMA to take care of."*

If I wanted to achieve my goal of getting that contract, I could not let these more educated men intimidate me. I could not afford to worry about THEIR qualifications, I had to concentrate instead on MY *goals*.

In the rest room, I reminded myself of my goals and then I returned to the boardroom. I walked bold. I looked good. I felt good. I smelled good. I sat down at that table and made my presentation and conducted my negotiations in a spirit of ABSOLUTE CERTAINTY.

I was *utterly* certain that the corporate officials involved had been BORN to give me that contract.

And I got the contract. Hello, Goal!

## Solid Goals

You must see your goals clearly and specifically before you can set out for them. Hold them in your mind until they become second nature. Before you go to bed each night visualize yourself accomplishing your goal. Do the same while you brush your teeth or take a shower in the morning.

Goals are not dreamy, pie-in-the-sky ideals. They have every-day practical applications and they should be practical. Your goals should be:

• *Well-defined.* You won't know if you've reached them if you haven't established exactly what they are.

• *Realistic.* Not that you can't be president some day, but shooting for state representative might be a wiser first step.

• *Exciting and meaningful to you.* Otherwise, where will your motivation come from?

- *Locked into your mind.*
- *Acted upon.* There is no sense in having a goal if you aren't going to go after it.

How do you find your goals? We all have dreams of what we would like to be doing, what we would like to have, who we would like to be with. Think about your dreams. What goal would you go after if you knew you would not fail? If you had unlimited funds? If you had infinite wisdom and ability?

One of the most essential things you need to do for yourself is to choose a goal that is important to you. If you need to set goals for your career, find a job or profession that is important to you beyond the bills that it pays.

It is vital to your growth as a person that your work is more than a job to you; that you have a higher purpose for doing what you do. I believe that sometimes we get into career paths or relationships that are really not what we want and then we struggle to make them work. As a result, we become frustrated and confused. We feel that we are working to no good purpose.

A woman told me once that when she went in to work at a job that she despised, it was like a refrigerator falling on her shoulders as soon as she stepped inside the door. She knew that she had gone as far as she would ever go in that job, and it weighed heavily on her. *Refrigerator heavy.*

She was stuck in that job and it was stuck on her. They were paying her just enough to keep her from quitting and she was working just hard enough to keep from getting fired. If you find yourself in that pattern, you must change your thinking and your behavior; otherwise you will continue to carry the weight of mediocrity on your shoulders.

## Enjoy the Pursuit

Find something you enjoy doing and build your goals around it. I was doing a seminar in Cleveland one time in which we tried to help people find things they loved to do. One of the participants, Berma, said she loved to bake cheesecakes. She was afraid we'd think that was silly, but we told her to write it down so we could brainstorm about how she could make money doing something she liked.

I don't believe that man was born to work for a living; I believe he was born to make what he lives for HIS WORK. We came up with a strategy for Berma and she called me a couple of weeks later and told me she'd quit her job.

She said, "I am baking cheesecakes every day and selling the cakes at twelve dollars each to specialty food stores throughout Cleveland." She began making a good living doing what she loved. She was in control of her life and loving it. What if her cheesecake business had failed? That's okay, because if you love what you are doing, at least you can enjoy the trip. George Burns said, "I would rather fail at what I love than succeed at what I hate."

Identify what you want to do and go after it. Assess your talents and then think of where they can take you. Write down the things you enjoy doing and how they might be turned into productive, marketable skills.

## Identify Your Talents and Nurture Them

You *do* have talents, you know. We all have things that we have a knack for and enjoy doing; *those are talents*. It is simply a matter of identifying them and developing them.

Do you get along well with people? Then you have a talent that can be channeled many ways. Public relations. Personnel training. Are you good with numbers? Accounting, income-tax preparation, bookkeeping, loan management, and banking are all possibilities for you. Are you musically inclined but not a particularly good musician? How about sound engineering? Band promotion? Record marketing? Jingle writing?

What do you *enjoy* doing? How can you do what you enjoy and make a living at it?

Most people never nurture their talents, skills and abilities. If you don't they will never serve you. I believe that each of us came here with something to give the world. Each of us has a unique offering. No one else is going to produce your product, write your book, open your academy. And if you don't bring your gift forward, if you die with it still inside you, then we all suffer from being deprived of your particular genius.

I heard a minister once say that the richest place on the planet is not some diamond mine or an oil field. It is a cemetery, because in the cemetery, we bury the inventions that were never produced, the ideas and dreams that never became reality, the hopes and aspirations that were never acted upon.

Most people take their dreams to the grave with them because they are fearful or they don't feel worthy or they listen to negative inner conversations instead of creating their own circumstances for success and exercising the power to change their lives. But if you tune out those voices, your talents—no matter how basic—will take you many places.

I like to talk. That is *a simple pleasure*. I'm good at it. A *common talent*. And yet I have worked as a door-to-door salesman, a disc jockey, a state representative and a public speaker. Without a college education, from a background of poverty, I have made a *very good* living by transforming my simple pleasure and my common talent into a career. My gifts have taken me to many places that I never dreamed I would get to go and given me access to audiences around the world.

You too have something that you brought to the universe. If you decide to develop what you do well and become a master of yourself, if you set goals and go after them with all the determination you can muster, your gifts will take you places that will *amaze* you.

## Your Reach Should Exceed Your Grasp

To accomplish great things, you must do as one of the great architects of Chicago, Daniel Burnham, advised: "Make no small plans." Think big when you set your goals. Dare to think big and then set a series of smaller goals to get you there. Your goals should go beyond your own material needs. They should be goals that serve your purpose while meeting a larger need in the world.

No one cares that you want money and a comfortable life. But they might care about what you have that would make *their* lives more comfortable, safer, or more fulfilling. Think big. Think mass market. I'll never forget the day I saw a beautiful big yacht with the word DRUM stenciled on its stern in a harbor in the Florida Keys. I asked a friend who lived there if he knew who owned it, and he said that he'd heard the owner was the guy who had patented the fifty-gallon drum. The next day, I saw another yacht, a huge one that was just as big as the house it was moored behind. "The guy who lives there developed the metal detectors that are used in airports," my friend said. What application of your natural abilities and talents would serve both your purpose and the needs of the marketplace? What could you do to make a difference in the world?

The options are vast. There are goals galore. I know of a young man named Christopher who earned a college degree in criminal justice and then tried to get a job in the security office of a large equipment manufacturer. No jobs. Then he applied to become a claims investigator for an insurance company. No jobs. He was down, but far from out.

Christopher lives in the Midwest where the hottest new recreational industry is riverboat gambling. He found out that the riverboat casinos had a great need for security management and there were very few people in the Midwest trained for that sort of work. Christopher went after it wholeheartedly.

As soon as he heard about the openings, he drove one hundred miles to apply for a job. He went back every day for a week. Always in a suit, shoes shined, looking good, feeling good. Eager to do it.

Christopher had some doubts, but he didn't let them show. He knew he lacked experience. He knew he was young. But he believed in his potential. The head of security got one look at Christopher and he said, "You are EXACTLY what we are looking for."

## Think of You, Inc.

Like many of us, Christopher had even more going for him than he had realized. When you think of yourself in the marketplace, envision yourself as a small corporation with assorted departments, with definite assets and liabilities. Christopher was inexperienced, sure, but he was also bright. He was fit. And he was *highly trainable*. They wanted fresh faces and clear minds that could be trained for a brand-new industry. They wanted people without preconceived notions.

Christopher not only got a job, he got a promotion before he even started work. And within a few months, he was promoted again. Now Christopher is one of the few young men in the Midwest with experience in security operations for riverboat casinos and more and more of these boats are going into operation all the time. His options are expanding and his opportunities are, too. And more important, he LOVES what he is doing. He is excited about it.

*There are goals galore out there*, no matter what your specific interests are. You are limited only by the limits on your ability to dream. And we can *all* dream.

## Seek Your Goals and They Will Find You

It might be of some consolation to you that perhaps the greatest motivator of all time, Dr. Norman Vincent Peale, the author of *The Power of Positive Thinking*, has said that HE had no motivation and no goals even as a college student.

He drifted along, without direction, not knowing what talent or what goals he had, until one day he went to a student-volunteer group meeting and entered a great hall where there hung a sign that read THE EVANGELIZATION OF THE WORLD IN THIS GENERATION.

That sign ignited a spark in him. He decided to be an evangelist whose message dealt not with heavenly rewards but with human potential. He wrote of this in *You Can If You Think You Can*. "I had my goal instantly formed, which was to do all that I could by whatever means to persuade and persuade and persuade people that they have built within them God-given and fantastic powers that, when released, can and will revamp them into significant personalities."

## Keep On Climbing Up

Reflect on your goals and evaluate your progress toward them regularly. I believe in constantly reevaluating my life and setting new goals as I achieve my old ones.

I think we should live, as the Reverend Robert Schuller says, *peak-to-peek*, conquering one peak and then peeking over the top to find another one to climb. Unless you want to wander through life without direction, you need to set goals and go after them, pickax in hand, aware that it may be a long and lonely climb.

As you reach your goals, set new ones. That is how you grow and become a more powerful person. How do you keep setting new goals? Let's say your goal was to get a job in your chosen field of law enforcement. Obviously, you should try to get at least an associate's degree in criminal justice or a related area. You do it. Goal achieved. Now what? On to the next goal. You'll probably have to start out near the bottom of the ladder as a jail or prison guard, a private security guard or investigator, a rookie police officer or sheriff's deputy.

What goal do you go to from there? After you've obtained a few years' experience, you will have a better idea of where you want to go in the field. Always know that it is possible for you to go after your goals and to live your dreams. It is essential that you be open to all of the possibilities that exist for you in this world.

## Live for the Possibilities

A boyhood friend of mine, Dwight Whyms, was rushed to the hospital with kidney failure, collapsed lungs and a failed liver. He was Code Blue.

His parents went into the emergency room and the doctor said, "I'm sorry, your son is dying."

His mother looked at her son. Then she looked at the doctor. "You have no right to say that," she asserted. "You are not God."

The doctor ran down the list of ominous signs. The liver and kidneys had failed. The lungs had collapsed. The heart had stopped beating twice and they had resuscitated him.

"But is there a possibility that he will live?" his mother demanded. "Has anybody else ever survived this sort of thing?"

The doctor allowed that yes, it was a possibility. "But it is not probable," he said.

The mother held her ground. This was her son.

"All I need to know, is it a possibility that he will survive?"

"Yes, it is possible," conceded the doctor, "but it is not probable."

"I don't care about probable," said Dwight's mother. "Just leave him alone."

His brother, Bou, my lifelong best friend, arrived at the hospital and he looked at Dwight, and he looked at his mother, and they both knew that it was possible that Dwight would survive. They knew with certainty because nineteen months earlier doctors had told Bou, "You have six months to a year to live."

At age forty-five, Bou was diagnosed with leukemia. The doctors gave him little hope. But he went after the possibilities. He went on a special diet, underwent blood transfusions, and he maintained a fighting spirit. Two years later, the leukemia was gone. And Bou is still here.

Bou is still my best buddy. Ever since he beat leukemia, he quotes a line from an old joke. "The doctor gave me six months to live, but I decided to take twenty years."

Certain that it was possible that Dwight might survive, Bou and other family members began a tireless campaign. They decided on a therapeutic technique that took advantage of one of the family's chief talents—talking.

They talked to Dwight while he was unconscious; they talked to him while he was asleep. They comforted him and encouraged him to fight.

Within three weeks, Dwight was walking and talking himself. They had instilled the fighting spirit in him. He survived.

As long as life holds forth possibilities, NO ONE can be counted out. Go after your goals. Live your dreams.

[See exercises for this chapter in the Action Planner on page 248.]

# Six

## Fix Your Focus

*People are always blaming their circumstances for what they are. I don't believe in circumstances. The people who get on in this world are the people who get up and look for the circumstances they want, and, if they can't find them, MAKE THEM.*

—GEORGE BERNARD SHAW

My mother wanted someone in life other than herself. Hers was a very basic goal. She had grown up without a mother and without siblings and so, as an adult, she yearned for the unselfish love of a family. She dreamed of it, and even though she no longer had a husband, she believed she could have it.

My mother was highly focused on her dream to have and support a family. I was nine years old and we were living in Overtown when she had a terrible accident that threatened her dream. She was working at the M & M Cafeteria as a cook, and one day she was moving a big pot of hot grease and lost control of it. Because of her arthritis she couldn't hold it up. She dropped it, and she spilled it on herself. All over her poor legs. She was badly burned.

Because of that accident, my mother lost her job and she was bedridden for weeks. After that, she could not work a regular job since her injuries, coupled with her arthritis, meant she could not move around too well. So she began taking in laundry and ironing.

At one point during her recovery, the only food we had in the house was a can of sardines that my sister had opened a few days earlier. She left it on a shelf in the refrigerator. I asked Mama if I could eat those sardines but she said no, that they might have spoiled.

Mama thought spoiled seafood could give me ptomaine poisoning but she knew I was hungry. "Bring the sardines to me," she said. "I will eat some of them first. If I get sick, you go call the neighbor, Miss Catherine. If I don't get sick, then you can have them."

I said, "No, Mama, that's okay, I'm not hungry."

But she insisted on doing that for me. She ate some of the sardines and my brother and sister and I stood vigil at her bedside. My brother was not as emotional as I was. He did not seem to be at all concerned. I think I came into this world with an old soul. I was praying, "Oh, Lord, please don't let Mama get sick." And I kept asking, "Mama, are you all right?"

She was perspiring. And she moaned and groaned in her sleep but apparently it was from the sickness that she already had because she opened her eyes after a while and said, "I'm all right, son."

And after a while longer, she told us that she had not suffered any from eating the sardines. So we devoured them, secure in the knowledge that if those old sardines didn't kill Mama, they surely would not kill us.

Whatever your dream or goal is, it is going to take the sort of commitment, dedication, drive, focus and faith my Mama brought to raising her adopted family.

## Build Confidence in Your Dream

Sometimes as you pursue your goal, it is difficult to make that mental leap from where you are to where you want to be. Grasping the magnificent possibilities that lie ahead demands a greatly expanded consciousness.

When faced with towering obstacles it might be too much of a stretch to say, "I can do that." You might be tempted instead to abandon the journey. To help you make that leap mentally, establish a benchmark—a place to go mentally where you can reflect and get your bearings.

Imagine a small room that makes you comfortable. A study, for example. Then, in your mind, go to it, sit down and relax and empower yourself with inner conversation. Erect a shelter from the self-doubt where you can pause and consider the possibilities of summoning the courage to continue. Draw strength by saying positive affirmations:

• "This is my decade. Nothing is going to stop me."
• "I know what I want in life and I will do whatever it takes to get it."
• "I have the power to handle whatever comes up."
• "I will move competently through my tasks today."
• "I am worthwhile and talented and I deserve my goals."
• "It is possible for me to live my dreams."

You must remain focused in your journey to greatness. Here are a few things to consider:

• In developing your plan, what kind of resources are you going to need?
• What are your long-range and short-range goals?
• Whom do you need to bring in to give you some assistance?
• What changes are required?

• Think about why your dream is important to you. What drives you?

• What will you do if your first plan of action does not work? Do you have a backup plan? What if that plan does not work?

Ask yourself these questions until the answers become clear. If you work with a problem long enough, it will begin to reveal its solutions to you. That is one of the powers you have within you.

So let's run down the game plan. You accept that life is going to be hard. You develop a plan of action to achieve your goals. You work on that plan relentlessly, and then I suggest you develop a three- to five-year strategy. Give yourself that much time before you demand results.

## Positive Visualization: Imagine Doing It and Do It

I believe that you are the director, the producer, the script-writer and the star of your own life. You decide whether it is going to be a smash or a flop. It is in your hands. When you are the *master* of your destiny, anything is within your reach.

A director envisions how he wants his movie to play out and then he pulls all the elements together to create that vision. Visualization can be helpful to you in focusing on your goals as well.

My friend Sarah practices a form of visualization when she goes house hunting. She looks until she finds a house in which she can envision her shoes in the closet. If she sees her shoes in the closet, she knows she'll get the house.

Sarah may not know it, but she is on the cutting edge. Visualization has become a major area of study in a number of fields. Visualization is another form of concentration and focus. Studies have shown that nearly all top athletes instinctively use visualization of some sort.

A quarterback goes back to pass and envisions a receiver breaking free and making a cut across the field on the thirty-yard line and catching the ball. Touchdown! A basketball player envisions himself making a move; he sees the opponent react to it, and the path to the basket clears. Two points!

Positive visualization is an effective method for programming the mind to succeed. It is a wonderful way in which to focus on your goals. And it doesn't just apply to athletics or Sarah's house hunting. It can work in a business setting, too.

Before going to work in the morning, take a few minutes to relax, maybe just before you get out of bed, or in the shower. Follow these steps.

• Run through a checklist of your arms, leg, back and neck muscles. See them relaxing. Feel them relax.

• Envision your workplace. Your office or surroundings. The sights and smells and sounds.

• Call to mind the tasks that you have to perform that day. Rank them in order of importance.

• Envision yourself doing each task with total concentration. Feel confidence and cheerfulness as you envision it. Feel fulfillment in doing each task well.

• As you envision each task, also work on your focus. Tell yourself that you will block out things happening around you, things that happened in the past or in the future.

• Remember, take each task from start to finish in your mind before beginning a new task.

• Envision your boss seeing your work and approving the manner in which you approached and completed each task.

• See yourself leaving the office at the end of the day in a good, satisfied mood, with all of your designated tasks completed.

Visualization can also be applied to the often anxious process of decision making in your work or in your personal life. The process is much the same with a few additional steps.

• Get into the relaxed state of mind again.

• Close your eyes and take your mind over all relevant information and materials.

• Staying relaxed, open your eyes, review all the relevant information. Go over each variable and each element that is affected by the decision. Know each alternative.

• Close your eyes again. Envision yourself choosing one of the alternatives. Play it out and see the results. Feel the emotions that come from having chosen that alternative.

  Do this with each alternative decision until you have gone through every possible scenario you can envision.

• Open your eyes and review what the results and emotions were in each alternative scenario. You should be ready now to make a decision with which you feel comfortable.

## Focus and Act on Your Dream

Whatever dream you decide to go after, whether it is a family, or a career goal, you must consciously decide that it is your *life's mission*. Benjamin Disraeli said, "The secret of success is constancy to purpose." You must go at it obsessively and set high standards for yourself along the way. There is no room for compromise when you are charting a course for your life or your career.

I spoke to a group of sharp young people not long ago, and when I finished, some of the fellows came up and said they were interested in becoming professional speakers. They invited me to go out with them that evening to have a good time. These fellows looked as though they knew how to have a *serious* good time.

I had planned to work on my delivery that night by listening to my tape of my speech. I tape my speeches and listen to them later so I can study what works and what does not work with a particular audience. In effect, I listen to the audience listening to me.

I was tempted to go with these fellows, and back when I was their age I probably would have given in to that temptation and gone. But I have become more disciplined and more committed to my craft.

A friend of mine, Wes Smith, wrote a humor book called *Welcome to the Real World*, and in it he offered advice to fresh high-school and college graduates. He had a line in the book that pertains to the situation I faced that night. It said, "Having a drink with the boys after work every night is a bad idea. Notice that the boss doesn't do it. That is why *he* is the boss and *they* are still the boys."

Wes told me that he wrote that line with one particular group of hard-partying young businessmen in mind, and five years after the book came out, he ran into one of them. The guy volunteered that he'd read that line in Wes's book and decided never to go drinking after work again. It paid off, he said. He had risen to a vice-presidency at a savings and loan.

In my drive to become a public speaker, I developed that kind of *focus*, too. There is not a lot of time for hard partying if you are pursuing greatness. It was not that these young fellows were not serious about their interest in professional speaking, but they were just as serious about having a good time. I don't believe they were focused on their goals. They were seeking a profession but they were not on a mission to make a dramatic difference in the world. I am. You should be too.

Rather than the party crowd, I prefer to seek out people with knowledge that might be useful. I like to find out what books successful and intelligent people are reading. I want access to the information that contributes to their success and intelligence.

## Assemble Your Life's Support System

When you embark on an unfamiliar and challenging journey, it often helps to take with you someone who knows the way, or at least someone familiar with this type of journey. When you determine where you want to go, or what you want to become in life, search for people along the way to become your life's support system.

Along the way I've had my mother, my lifelong friend Bou, my teacher Mr. Washington and, in more recent years, my friend and adviser Mike Williams.

These are not people you pick up along the way. These are people who pick *you* up along the way. Bou is a lifelong friend who has been there through my marriages and divorces, through the rearing of my children. He is a person who often sees my needs before I do. Mr. Washington, you know about him. He gave my life a positive sense of direction. Mike Williams took me to another level. When I was a popular disc jockey at a station in Columbus, Mike came to me and convinced me that my natural talents at communicating could serve a higher purpose. He told me that rather than simply entertaining people, I could enlighten them and empower their lives with my gift for communicating.

I have come to believe that, to a certain degree, when the student is ready, the teacher appears. I first met Mike when I attended a meeting at which he spoke. I was impressed with his intelligence and articulate presentation. We became friends and Mike came to see things in me that I did not see in myself. Through his patience and example, he helped me reach a higher level. It has not always been easy for either of us. Mike is hard on me sometimes, and I have been known to be a somewhat inattentive pupil.

When I became a program director at the radio station, I hired Mike to work as my news director. I was still undisciplined at that time in my life, and I liked to sneak out of the office to shoot pool now and then. Mike made me feel guilty about it, so I would duck down and duck-walk past his office window. Sometimes he'd catch me in the parking lot and say, "Brown! Where are you going?" I wanted to be in broadcasting at that point, but I wasn't committed enough to be in the building all day long being focused on my goal. I was creative, but I didn't like to keep my nose to that grindstone.

Mike convinced me that there were greater possibilities for my humble gifts than being a radio entertainer. He had a greater vision of what I could do to help others, and he has stayed with me to keep me on the path that he first envisioned. He developed the nine principles for life enrichment. He is a beacon that lights my way.

I believe that as you grow in consciousness you begin to attract people who facilitate your growth. Be on the lookout for these sorts of people, the masters, the mentors and the people who see things for you that you do not see for yourself. Find those who can look at your performance objectively and critically but positively.

We all need to have friends who hold our feet to the fire and challenge us. You need mutually enhancing relationships. As my relationship with Mike developed, he imparted some of his work habits to me. Look for the sort of friends who help you work on your weaknesses, not just those who feed your habits and congratulate you on your strong points.

Once I moved into the realm of public speaking, I sought out more specific guides. I began corresponding with Norman Vincent Peale and other giants in the public-speaking field. I learned from those who had gone the way I wanted to go, and succeeded. Think of the problems I avoided because THEY had encountered and had overcome them. Think of the experiences I picked up just by communicating.

You can seek mentors in all aspects of your life, not just your work. Another of my goals was to become a better father. I'd thought that paying the bills and buying clothes and picking the children up and taking them places and doing things with them was enough.

But I discovered it is one thing to give a check, it is a much greater thing to give *yourself*. Sharing who you are is one of the most vital things a parent offers a child.

We all need to seek role models and develop relationships with them. We need to be especially conscious of our abilities as parents because it is our responsibility to build purpose in our children.

And I believe that by actively pursuing your dreams, you may be extending the time you have to be with your children and grandchildren and great grandchildren.

The number-one killer in this country is heart disease. And the majority of people suffer their first major heart attack *on Monday morning between eight and nine.* That is the time, of course, when most people are getting ready to go to jobs that they don't like, jobs that are making them sick.

When you are not pursuing your goal in life, when you are unfulfilled and just cruising along unconsciously, I believe that you are literally committing spiritual suicide.

In pursuing your goals, you have to be conscious of yourself, and of the world around you. You need a *global* vision. You need to do your homework. Study all the factors that influence and are affected by your area of interest. Benjamin Franklin said, "If a man empties his purse into his head, no one can take it away from him. An investment in knowledge always pays the best interest."

When you understand the marketplace, you will have a better feel for the motivations of your employers. You may be surprised to learn that many farmers have computers in their homes now so that they have access to the latest grain and commodity prices around the world. Farmers know their market. They know that after they haul their grain to a nearby grain elevator, it is shipped by rail or truck to a barge line which moves it on the water to destinations around the world.

Farmers are well aware that world events affect the value of crops in their fields and the livestock in their feed lots.

They know that a bad winter in the wheat fields of Eastern Europe will impact on their farms in Kansas and Nebraska. They understand that they are linked to a global economy. You need to understand that, too.

The success of CNN is not mere happenstance. We are no longer a nation of isolated and independent interests. We are globally connected. What are the economic, social and political forces that affect your area of interest? Who are the primary competitors? What are the innovators doing? What is the latest trend in education in your field?

## Speak the Language

When I give a speech to a group, I always make an effort to sit down with its representatives and discuss with them all the factors involved in their profession. I ask them to send me trade magazines beforehand. People empowered by their dreams seek out information. They are THAT focused. They laser in on their goals.

When I address a group, I want to know what economic factors come into play in their field. I want to know whether their business is in an up or down cycle. I ask the executives what it is they want from their employees. I ask the employees what it is they want from their executives.

I want to speak their own language to them, not some generic memorized speech that has only token references to their area of interest. I tailor my speeches even as I am giving them so the audience knows I am geared to their needs.

That *holistic* approach—a study of the whole field—accelerated my growth in professional speaking but it will work for you, as well.

Your ability to communicate is an important tool in your pursuit of your goals, whether it is with your family, your co-workers or your clients and customers. How do you rate yourself as a communicator? Do you work well with people? Are you open to feedback? Can you get others to share your vision? Can you motivate them beyond their perceived limits? Can you get them to cross the street with you?

As the world, and the United States in particular, evolves from an industrial society into a service-driven economy, communication is rapidly becoming the most vital tool you can have.

I know of a man who has a key position in a large accounting firm in Chicago even though he has never studied accounting. He has a master's degree in English literature, and many people regard him as the only person in his corporation who speaks English. His job is to take all the numbers and facts compiled by the accountants and communicate the findings of the bean-counters to their customers. He writes the final reports. He is the designated communicator, and he makes a good living at it.

I was reminded of the importance of communications skills when I observed a press conference a few years ago with Sugar Ray Leonard and his opponent Tommy "Hit Man" Hearns. The difference between the earning power of the two fighters is enormous, and it is almost entirely because of the fact that Sugar Ray Leonard is a superb communicator. Because of his charismatic, articulate personality, he won promotional contracts worth millions even when he lost in the ring.

You need to note that communication does not mean simply the ability to verbalize your thoughts. God gave us two ears and one mouth, and that means we are expected to listen twice as much as we talk. Are you a good listener? Do you ask questions that help the other person become a better communicator? Do people feel comfortable around you, or do you dominate conversations?

Even if you are highly motivated, you won't get anywhere if you can't communicate that to the essential people.

## High Standards for High Achievement

When you take control of your life and work toward a goal it pulls you out of your *comfort zone*—that's the place where you are content to just cruise along without demanding anything of yourself or of life. You need to get out of that idling existence to tap your talents and abilities and achieve your goals. Ask yourself if you are leaving a trail that others may want to follow. Are you leaving a legacy of accomplishment? What mark will you leave on your industry? Your friends and family?

There is also the matter of setting high standards in what you do. Too many people do not consider this, but I believe that the public is becoming increasingly demanding in this regard.

I recently pulled into a service station that was very busy. There were two cars in front of me and, soon, two cars behind me. The station attendant was obviously harried. He was taking a credit-card transaction from the first car. But he completely ignored the other cars in line. If he had just bothered to look up and acknowledge the other drivers, they probably would have been patient with him. I know I would have done that in exchange for a little courtesy, a show of appreciation for my business. But he did not make that effort, and we all left to find another station.

People do not want to be treated as if they are invisible. They want it recognized that their business is valuable. I believe that is one reason that at a time when many large department stores are declaring bankruptcy, the Nordstrom's chain based in Seattle is opening elegant stores around the country.

Nordstrom's is known for its innovative customer relations. Its sales people are trained to meet high standards of courteous and personal service. They even offer live piano music in each store, rather than the usual canned Muzak. I find it remarkable that most of the major newspapers in the country have done stories on Nordstrom's simply because it devotes so much attention to the quality of its customer service.

It seems to me that customer service should be a given in any business, but apparently it has become such a lost art that its revival makes for big news.

## Seek Excellence

I travel a great deal and I generally go back to those hotels in which the staff offers the best service. I am impressed when the chambermaids offer me a "Good morning." An associate of mine who came to Detroit to meet with me recently was highly impressed that his hotel offered free limousine service to and from any destination he needed to reach in the city.

The hotel management obviously valued his business. In fact, at one point an assistant manager drove him to my office because the bellmen were all busy. That hotel is more expensive than many others in town and it is not centrally located, but he will go back there and he will tell many others about the fine treatment he received and the high standards of the staff.

I know a Realtor who does not have an especially dynamic personality but she sells millions in real estate each year because of her high standards. She believes that if she puts the customer first, she will never come in second to another Realtor. Ninety-nine percent of her business is repeat or referral.

Not everyone seems to be getting the message that service is the key, however. I spoke recently to a group of American automobile dealers and salesmen, and frankly, I was greatly saddened by some of the things I heard while I was in their company. They devoted a great deal of time and energy to creatively bashing and mocking their foreign competitors.

I believe that energy and creativity would be far better employed in setting high standards in their product and service. No runner ever won a race by looking over his shoulder and demeaning the competition.

You have to concentrate on what you can do to make your product or your pitch or your talents absolutely irresistible. You do that by setting high standards and by constantly upping the ante.

It seems to me that for decades American automakers had the attitude "If it's not broke, don't fix it." Their foreign competitors, on the other hand, seemed to believe, "If it's not perfect, keep working on it."

This is a customer-driven economy and if we are going to maintain our edge, we must take the attitude that our goal is to AMAZE people with our product and our service.

## Be Dedicated to Achieving Your Dreams

You cannot gain on your goal with an attitude that you will pursue it only if it is convenient, or as long as there are no hassles, or no hoops to jump through. Life is not that kind of party. It is a rough go out there.

I advise you to say your dream is possible and then overcome all inconveniences, ignore the hassles and take a running leap through the hoop even if it is in flames. A late friend of mine named Bob Mays once wrote a song called "Don't Let NOBODY Turn You Around."

You need to be open to the *possibilities* out there too. Look for *opportunities* that exist in your current place of employment. At a time when no job is secure in this country, it benefits you to become indispensable. It is important for you to learn all there is to learn about your particular field because that will give you an edge. I believe you need to always work for that edge.

When asked to perform extra duties at work, unfocused people say, "That is not in my job description." That is not the proper attitude in this day and age. You need to do and to know all that you possibly can in order to make yourself indispensable—if you want to continue working where you are.

When I first got into broadcasting my primary interest was in being a disc jockey, but I set about learning everything I could about every aspect of the business. I became a broadcasting sponge. And during my career I ultimately did it all. I served as music, program and production director. I produced and directed commercials. I sold airtime. I put together concert shows and was master of ceremonies. I believe people must become multi-talented and multi-skilled to make it in today's market.

I started out as an errand boy and I believe that you must be prepared to pay your dues in any line of work. You may have to sweep floors to get in the door, but once you are inside, you have far more opportunities than if you were still on the outside. The Greek statesman Demosthenes said, "Small opportunities are often the beginnings of great enterprise."

I know of a man who wanted to be a sound technician for recording studios. He got a college degree in sound engineering and then he traveled around the country trying to get a job. He discovered that it was a tightly knit fraternity that was difficult to break into.

The only job he was offered by a recording studio was that of janitor. They told him that many of their people—even those with degrees—had started that way. It was a very famous recording studio, and he was tempted, but because he had built up so much debt getting his degree, he turned it down. For many years after that, he wished he had taken that low-level job because he realized it would have gotten him in the door.

Even sweeping floors is not such a bad job if it puts you closer to your dream. It is only a bad job if it is taking you nowhere.

## Pursue Your Dream Because You Deserve It

Go after your dream with a sense of entitlement. Know that you have the power to achieve it and that you deserve it. Be willing to get up into life's face, grab it by the collar and say, "Give it UP! It's my dream."

Whatever you accomplish in life is a manifestation not so much of what you *do*, as of what you believe deeply within yourself that you *deserve*.

You have to focus on yourself and sell yourself on your ability to perform, to achieve your objectives and to *deserve* them. Tell yourself when you review your goals each day, that you deserve them. Say to yourself, *"I'm capable, talented; I'm committed. I DESERVE my goals."*

I once had a goal of being featured in *Ebony* magazine. It wasn't prompted by any egotistical desire to see my name or my picture in print. I believed it was important to get my message of self-determination out to the readers of that magazine.

I focused *my* life-force on Mr. John H. Johnson, the publisher of that magazine. His *secretary's* life-force resisted, so I dialed his telephone number time and time again for two years. I did not know Mr. Johnson personally, so I started asking everyone I knew if THEY knew of him or of anyone who knew him.

As the founder of Johnson Publications, he is, I believe, one of the greatest entrepreneurs in this country. He truly had to overcome incredible odds to produce the financial empire he has created with *Ebony* and *Jet* magazines, Fashion Fair Cosmetics, two radio stations, a syndicated television show, the Supreme Life Insurance Company and other enterprises. Mr. Johnson's fortune has been estimated at $500 million, and I think it is all the more valuable by virtue of what he had to overcome.

He was a native of Arkansas City, Arkansas; his mother worked as a maid after they came to Chicago and was on welfare for a time. He took out a $500 loan, using his mother's furniture as collateral, to start his first magazine, *Negro Digest*. Mr. Johnson is entirely a self-made man. He had to overcome a great deal to succeed. As George Washington Carver said, "Judge a man not by what he has but what he had to overcome to make his accomplishment."

One of the things Mr. Johnson says that has inspired me and I think others of similar backgrounds is: "There is no defense against an excellence that meets a pressing public need."

That thought inspired me to keep after him, as did this other quote attributed to him: "I believe . . . that living on the edge, living in and through your fear, is the summit of life, and that people who refuse to take that dare condemn themselves to a life of living death."

I took the dare, and eventually someone gave me Mr. Johnson's private telephone number and I called him and talked with him. I wanted him to see me speak. He said he had no interest and he hung up.

*Oh, good,* I thought, *ANOTHER dare!*

I didn't take it personally. I kept pursuing my goal. As it happened, when I spoke to a group in Cleveland a person in the audience came forward and said, "You've been calling me about hooking you up with Mr. Johnson at *Ebony*. I will make it possible for you to speak at a function that he will attend."

I spoke at that function and Mr. Johnson was there. I *burned* the place up. And Mr. Johnson ordered an article done on me and my message.

If you want to make it happen, you have to be relentless. I once had another goal of appearing on the syndicated television show of the Reverend Robert Schuller. I telephoned an associate producer of the show, who put up resistance.

"You're not an author of a book, are you?"

"Not yet," I replied.

"You're not a celebrity," she noted.

"No, but if you put me on your program, I will become one. I'm a *very* good guest."

"I'm sorry," she said, "we are not in the business of *making* people celebrities."

"OK, no problem," I said, "but I have a good message that would benefit your viewers."

"I'm *sure* you do, sir; everyone who calls here does. Contact us when you do something of *national significance*."

My energy was not the least bit depleted. It was still charging. I just plugged in to someone else with the show. I found someone who sounded sympathetic to my cause. I sent her tapes. I called her. I developed a relationship with her over the telephone. It took me a year and a half, but I never stopped. I was *MR. UNSTOPPABLE*. I envisioned myself on that program and I directed my energy at realizing that vision.

I was speaking before a company in Chicago and I learned that the president of that company, Mr. George Johnson of Johnson Products, had once donated a million dollars to the Robert Schuller ministry. It dawned on me that such a donor might have influence enough to get me onto the program. After I delivered a speech that had his employees EXCITED about their jobs, I approached the president of the company and asked for his help getting on the Schuller program. He said he would do it. He wrote a letter and I got the phone call inviting me to be on.

Without a book, without celebrity, without doing anything of national significance, I got on. Just me, Mrs. Mamie Brown's baby boy.

Her *unstoppable* baby boy.

## Be Unstoppable

You cannot be wimpy out there on the dream-seeking trail. Dare to break through barriers, to find your own path.

For years and years it was said that no man would ever

run the mile in less than four minutes. And then Roger Bannister, a physician and graduate of Oxford University, transcended the conventional experience. He followed his inner vision, his dreams, and in 1954, he ran the mile in 3.59.4 minutes.

Bannister broke through a barrier, and *twenty thousand* have done it since, including high-school students. Why not before? Because people believed it couldn't be done.

After Bannister did it, his achievement challenged others to do the same thing. If anybody has ever done what you wanted to do or had a dream and made it come true, it is possible that you can, too. You must believe that.

It takes someone with a *vision of the possibilities* to attain new levels of experience. Someone with the courage to live his dreams.

I have a little affirmation, written by author Berton Braley, that I say at times when I need to build up my courage and to focus on my dreams and goals. Say this when you need to do the same.

> *If you want a thing bad enough to go out and fight for it, to work day and night for it, to give up your time, your peace and your sleep for it . . . if all that you dream and scheme is about it, and life seems useless and worthless without it . . . if you gladly sweat for it and fret for it and plan for it and lose all your terror of the opposition for it . . . if you simply go after that thing you want with all of your capacity, strength and sagacity, faith, hope and confidence and stern pertinacity . . . if neither cold, poverty, famine, nor gout, sickness nor pain, of body and brain, can keep you away from thing that you want . . . if dogged and grim you beseech and beset it, with the help of God, you WILL get it!*

[See exercises for this chapter in the Action Planner on page 252.]

# Seven

# Fear of Frogs

*Nothing is so much to be feared as fear.*
—HENRY DAVID THOREAU

As a young boy, I sometimes accompanied my mother when she worked for extra money as a farm laborer in the tomato fields of southern Florida. In those dry, dusty fields, under a sun that seemed to grow more intense as it sapped the life-force from the bent backs of men, women and children, Mama picked alongside migrants from Mexico, the Bahamas and Jamaica.

As a child, I was fairly oblivious to the plight of the migrant workers, just as I was relatively unaware of my family's own economic poverty. But I dreaded going into those tomato fields for they harbored creatures that I feared more than anything else in my childhood.

Yes, I am talking about the leaping terror of my youth: MY FEAR OF FROGS. I was a true amphibiphobe. I was so terrified of frogs that every time I saw one, I ran as if I'd encountered a demon. You see, someone had told me that I could get warts from frogs. And warts were definitely not on my personal grooming agenda.

My Mama tried to tell me that there was nothing wrong with frogs. Snakes maybe. But not frogs. She said toads gave you warts, anyway, not frogs. But I was not convinced. I'd say, "I don't want to get those big bumps on me!"

There were not many distractions for the workers as they toiled sunup to sunset in the tomato fields, unless little Les Brown happened to be around. Word spread quickly that I was seriously scared of frogs and the workers amused themselves by teasing me. They would shout that a frog was headed my way and then watch me panic.

I was an easy mark. At the mere mention of a frog in my vicinity, I would take off in a mad scramble from the wart-carriers. When you scramble in a tomato field, you inevitably squash a lot of ripe produce. And when you squash produce in a tomato field, you cost someone money, which does not make the foreman happy at all.

So, you see, those frogs really did get me in trouble, but it wasn't because of anything THEY did to me, it was because of what I allowed them to do to me.

More than once, I got my butt whupped for smashing tomatoes because I was running from a fear that could cause me no real harm. Well, I know now what a silly fear that was, but it is no more silly than many of those meaningless fears we pick up as adults.

We often cause ourselves great trouble because of fears that, in reality, are no more worthy of our anguish than those FIENDISH FIELD FROGS OF FLORIDA!

We all need to step back and evaluate the fears that we carry into adulthood. Those childhood fears of a darkened room, a tree scraping the window or a thunderstorm give way to adult fears of business failure, personal rejection or financial instability, but often the fear does us more harm than the actual difficulties we inevitably face in life.

Look at the fears that may be hurting you needlessly or impeding your growth. Are they really worth what you have invested in them? Or are they baseless fears that you can abandon and move on from?

Too many of us are not living our dreams because we are living our fears. Too many of us never realize our full potential because our fears block us. What fears are keeping you from breaking out and living up to your full potential, from being truly happy and finding adventure and excitement in your life and controlling your own destiny?

## Fears Without Teeth

Psychiatrists say that there are only two fears that we are born with, and the fear of frogs—I am here to report—is not one of them. One is the fear of falling and the other is the fear of a loud sound. All other fears are learned. The fear of failure is a learned fear. So is the fear of success. These are two of the most crippling fears we must deal with in life.

Fear is an emotion, and like any mere emotion it can be controlled. I have heard the word *fear* defined as an acronym: "False Expectations Appearing Real." We are often victimized more by the false expectation than by the reality.

There was a boy who was victimized by his neighbor's bulldog. Every day when the boy left his home this dog chased him. He would run for his life with the bulldog at his heels. But one day the boy got plain tired of running. He decided he had run enough.

When the bulldog came after him, he picked up a rock and cocked his arm to throw it. That stopped the dog in his tracks. The bulldog kept his distance, but he began barking. And then the boy saw something that shocked him. That bulldog had no TEETH! He was as toothless as a laying hen! *The only thing that dog could have done to him was gum him to death!*

That boy realized then that he had been running from a baseless fear. We all have faced similar situations in life. We discover that we have been fearful of something that in truth has no power to hurt us. Our False Expectations Appeared Real, but they were not.

Of course, some people take delight and refuge in frightening themselves. There is a certain perverse comfort in the emotion of fear. That explains why so many of us went to see *The Exorcist*.

I will never forget seeing that movie. I was so frightened by it that I called my former wife from a pay phone on the way home and said, *"Turn the garage and house lights on for me, will you?"*

Even when I got home I found myself paralyzed in the car. I could not get out. I started honking the horn, calling for my former wife. "Madelyn, they've got me! They've got me!"

She came to the window and said, "Fool! Take your seat belt off!" I was frightened out of my wits. *By my seat belt!*

I think I must have wanted to be afraid. Sometimes our fears reassure us that we are alive, even as they keep us from really living. The psychologist Abraham Maslow said that we must face our fears in order to live fully. He advised: "You can turn back, but if you want to grow you must be willing to go forward and face your fears again and again and again."

We will never experience a fear-free existence. We never have. Man has been chased by his fears from the start of human history. It may no longer be *Tyrannosaurus rex* that you fear is on your tail, but it may be the I.R.S.

## Better Fears Than Tears

Fear then, is natural, and not entirely unhealthy. There are things that you should be afraid of. That is why mothers teach their children to be fearful of putting their fingers on the gas burners or of sticking straight pins into electrical outlets.

Good healthy fear serves a purpose; it protects us from danger—as anyone who has burned a finger or been jolted by a few hundred volts knows. The fear of bodily harm is a legitimate fear.

When I was twenty-two or twenty-three years old, I

thought I was a pretty tough streetwise guy, until there came an occasion when I had to confront one of those legitimate fears. I was a disc jockey on WVKO, a Columbus, Ohio, radio station and I heard about some guy who was going around town passing himself off as the singer Al Green.

Now, I had booked Al Green at concerts in the area and I knew him. So when I learned of this imposter I did an editorial on my show and exposed him and told people not to pay him any money or give him anything for free.

This imposter was a fairly streetwise fellow himself, a LARGE fellow too, and he put the word out on the street that he was going to knock Les Brown in his big mouth.

*Fearlessly*, I accepted the challenge and went looking for him. I was driving down Main Street and spotted him. I got out of the car and said, "I heard you were looking for me. I'm Les Brown. I'm the one who said you are an imposter. I want to know what you are going to do about it."

*Fearlessly*, he opened his overcoat and showed the handgun he had holstered beneath it. I recognized my fears immediately and I *embraced* them.

"Whatever I said to hurt your feelings, I apologize," I told him. And then I got back in my car and got out of there.

Yes, sir, acknowledge those fears, carry yourself accordingly, and do what makes the most sense for you. In this case, it made sense to grovel, grin and git. Hello, fear! Goodbye, Mister Imposter!

## Don't Let Fear Control You

There are times when you should proceed with caution in life. But there is a tremendous difference between having fear and *fear having you*. Many of us tend to make our fears more powerful than our dreams. You can accept fear as an emotion, even as a fact, but not as a force *to hold you back*.

Fear does not have any special power unless you empower it by submitting to it. You can accept that you are afraid and then move on. Fear does not have to become your reality.

I have a friend who scuba-dives. When he started, it unnerved him to be underwater breathing through his mouth with only the sound of his own labored breath in his ears. Then he learned that he could relax and ease his sense of panic merely by monitoring the sound of his breathing and controlling it.

By forcing himself to take steady, measured breaths, he overcame his anxiety in the strange environment. He conquered his fears by heightening his consciousness and seizing control. Scuba-diving became a joy for him, in large part because he took pride in mastering his initial fears and instinctive panic.

Of course, the first time a big shark cruised near him, panic set in and his breathing went back out of control. But that only provided yet another challenge and a new level of consciousness to master: *Jaws Consciousness*.

In mastering his fear while diving, he put into practice this maxim: *What you resist will persist. But what you embrace you can control.* Some fears, however, are less easily controlled than those related to physical danger. Such fears are often even more daunting and oppressive because they are more mentally than physically based. I'm referring to fears such as that of alienating someone you love while honestly trying to help them.

## Lost Love

Parents encounter this fear often. They fear disciplining their children will alienate them even though they realize that children need to learn discipline to survive in the world.

It is difficult, but there comes a time when parents must accept that their child may hate them for doing the right thing. Often children lack the maturity to appreciate the situation and parents have to exhibit the courage to confront them and guide them.

One of my sons got off on the wrong track awhile back. His overall behavior showed a level of immaturity that was eventually going to be detrimental. He was enrolled at Ohio State University and I was paying the tab. He began missing classes and his grades slipped.

By continuing to finance his education, I was reinforcing that negative behavior. I could not afford to do that if my son was to grow emotionally, mentally and spiritually. And so I told him, "I am not going to subsidize Ds and Fs. You either bring your grades up to a minimum B, or you pay your own tab."

He was upset with that ultimatum. But I was upset at myself for having been a wimpy parent. Because I challenged him, my son did not speak to me for a long period of time, but eventually he came back and apologized. I was afraid of losing him, but in fact, we became closer because I cared enough to confront him and set him straight.

The next semester, he dug in and got all Bs and As. Had I not confronted the situation, he probably would have continued to muddle through. What if he had simply given up and dropped out of school? Well, so be it. He is a grown man. He must learn to fly on the strength of his own wings.

## Fears with Teeth

I have not always been so successful in confronting things I dread. In fact, when it came to my fear of dentists, I fed the fear. I wallowed in it. I even sat through the movie *Marathon Man*, in which Sir Laurence Olivier portrays a Nazi torturer who gets Dustin Hoffman into a dentist chair and attempts to drill secrets out of him, molar by molar.

When Olivier went into Hoffman's mouth with that drill, my dollar's worth of popcorn went flying everywhere. But the movie served a purpose. It fed my fears to the point that I refused to see a dentist for five years.

Finally an impacted wisdom tooth got my attention. Even then, I procrastinated for weeks. I would telephone the dentist's office and hang up. Then I progressed to the point where I would schedule an appointment but in someone else's name, "Joe D. Doe," and then I'd break it. Or I'd schedule it in my own name and then claim pressing business prevented me from going through with it.

Eventually, the receptionist confronted my fears for me.

"You're scared, aren't you?" she said.

"That's *none* of your business," I retorted.

"Well, I wish you would stop wasting our time."

Meanwhile, back in my mouth, the wisdom tooth worsened. I had to do something. I had to handle it. I had to convince myself that the drill was not going to kill me or force me to betray any national secrets.

And once I gave myself over to the dentist, it really was not as bad as I had envisioned. I was delighted, not to mention relieved.

That often happens when you confront your fears. I am sure you have experienced a similar breakthrough at some point in your life. You dreaded doing something, you envisioned the worst unfolding, and then, when it was over, you had survived relatively intact. No mortal wounds. No lasting damage.

I have developed a technique to conquer my fears in these situations. I envision the worst-case scenario. I imagine that the dentist goes into my mouth with his drill and I pass out. That's the worst. And then I envision myself going in to the dentist and handling it calmly, and I play that vision over and over again in my mind until I feel and experience the confidence of handling that situation.

It is a method of focusing that force of consciousness. For years, I had a tremendous fear of speaking to "educated audiences," and as you can imagine, that greatly impeded my development as a public speaker. I am not college-trained and I had developed the notion that college graduates were so intelligent that I could not possibly have anything worth relating to them.

At a time when I was still struggling with this fear, I was asked to speak at a college commencement ceremony. My negative inner conversations were running a mile a minute and my confidence was lagging in the distance. "There is absolutely no way that you can connect with this audience. They will boo you off the stage. They will talk right through your speech." I was programming myself for failure.

## Visualize Victory

I made matters worse by taking a peek at the audience. There were hundreds of brainy college graduates out there. They had their magna cum laude diplomas in their hands. Panic set in. I told someone that I could not go on.

My chest tightened. My breaths came in short gasps. I was unconsciously sabotaging this moment that I had worked for. I was in the grip of my fears. And then something inside me said, "You have got to get a handle on this."

I found a friend and asked him to pray with me. And I remembered someone had once advised me to try visualization in these situations. So the first thing I did was visualize the worst that could happen. I saw myself fainting onstage. Then I started laughing at myself and I said, "See yourself handling it." I calmed myself down.

I visualized the audience giving me wildly enthusiastic applause. I visualized them nodding in agreement and inspiration at my wise, witty and wondrous presentation until I got a confident feeling. And in that manner, I conquered my fear. Magna cum laude.

I call this method, which several other people have told me they employ, my "As If" visualization. I visualized the scenario as if I had won the audience over already and then I just followed that positive path.

See yourself confronting your fears in your mind's eye and handling those fears like a champ. Tell yourself that you are MORE than able. I have since employed this process in various aspects of my life, even in dealing with difficult relationships.

Willie was a friend of mine, and he was an alcoholic. We had a mutual understanding. I pretended not to know of his alcoholism and he pretended not to know that I knew. It was a typical *male* relationship.

I had long been afraid of bringing the subject up because I did not want to endanger our friendship. But there came a point when his alcoholism endangered not only our relationship but his life as well. And I finally realized that I had to confront him openly. A mutual friend prodded me, "If you really love him and care about him, why don't you let him know so that he can get some help?"

I had to agree, and I began visualizing the approach I would take. I envisioned telling him that I felt he had a drinking problem, and I envisioned Willie telling me to go to hell. It could destroy our friendship, I knew.

I had to ask myself if I could live with that. I played that mental tape over and over. And in some reels I saw my friend responding angrily but I envisioned myself handling it.

When I finally did confront him in reality, I had my opening line ready. "Willie, I need to have a serious conversation with you. You have a problem with alcohol. I would like to be a support to you in dealing with it." Willie denied that he had a drinking problem. But I was strong. He was someone I cared for very much and I had admired him greatly. He had been a tremendous influence in my life. I had to take him on. When he continued his denials, I stepped closer and I said, "Yes, you do have a problem and I want to help you with it."

After a long struggle both within himself and with me, Willie conceded. He agreed to get some help. I went home drained. It was an agonizing confrontation but it was not as bad as I had envisioned.

Another friend, who was in Vietnam, said that when he faces a fearful situation, he summons up images of his war experiences and says to himself, "If I handled Vietnam, I can handle this." It takes no little courage to call up painful moments from the past but those deeply rooted experiences can become powerful tools for the positive side.

Another approach is employed often by people who are motivated by negative consequences. They ask themselves, "What is the negative impact of my not handling this? If I continue to put this off, what will happen?" In this case, the negative repercussions of their inaction or their submission to their fears propel them to take positive action.

## Making Difficult Decisions

And a final fear-beating method I've identified involves writing down three strong reasons why you must move past your fears and take action. I relied on this method myself when I had to fire one of my employees. I did not want to do it. I even took the decidedly cowardly approach of ordering my business manager to do it for me. I was going to leave town to avoid the fireworks. I like being the good guy. I was a wimp about this.

But finally, pride got the better of my wimpiness. I decided I had to handle the firing myself. So I wrote down three reasons why I needed to fire this employee. And as I read those reasons, I realized that they were valid and that firing the person was my only choice. I had been more than fair with him.

I called the employee into my office and I said, "Listen, you know I care about you and we've been together for a long time and even though I appreciate everything that you have done for me, here is what we both know. This is not working. We don't have to stop being friends but you can no longer work here. If there is any way that I can help you, I will. But I am telling you right now that I must let you go."

I ran that little speech through my mind over and over before I called the employee in. Even then, it was rough because we had been like relatives. But I felt much better for having done it myself rather than passing it off on someone else. And it was not as bad as I thought. I did not curl up and die.

## Know Your Value

Building your feelings of self-worth is critical to overcoming your fears. You need to remind yourself often that you are a worthwhile person and that you deserve to achieve your dreams and goals. You must see that in your mind's eye and know that you have what it takes, that you will persevere.

Many women find themselves in relationships that tear down their sense of self-worth. My friend Maria married a very controlling man. She came from a family with traditional values in which the woman's role was to support her husband and to care for their children. So she let herself be controlled and dominated. She paid a price. Her husband did not treat her as a partner in the marriage; he treated her more as a servant. This went on for decades, but after their children had grown up and gone out on their own, Maria began to assert her independence. As she was seeing her daughter off to college, Maria cautioned her that in her relationships with men, she should try to retain her own sense of purpose and self-worth. Her daughter, sensing that her mother was about to reassert herself, said, "Mama, it's your time."

So many people, particularly women, lose themselves when they devote their lives to their families. Maria began thinking of the dreams and goals she had suppressed in order to get along in her marriage to a domineering man. She discovered that her dreams had been dormant, but they were still strong. She began looking for her own happiness, rather than focusing entirely on what made HIM happy. As she grew out of the passive role and got back in touch with her own emotions, Maria realized that she had long been angry and resentful both toward her husband for treating her like property, and toward herself for becoming so subservient and allowing him to treat her so badly.

Maria had suffered a great many health problems in previous years, and she realized too that she probably had allowed her anger to wear down her good health. She had lost her fight, physically and mentally. Now, as a result of becoming an active force in her life, she changed the direction of it.

If you allow your self-esteem to erode, your fear will eat at you; ultimately it could destroy you. Eleanor Roosevelt had her own method for handling fears of trying something new. She said, "I believe that anyone can conquer fear by first doing three things: Do it once to prove to yourself that you can do it. Do it the second time to see whether or not you like it. And then do it again to see whether or not you want to keep on doing it." She said that by the time you have accomplished the third step, you are through the fear. You have handled it.

## Dare to Be Unpopular

Another type of fear we all have to learn to deal with is our fear of rejection or the fear that people might not like us. It is frightening to consider how many people do things simply out of fear of offending someone else.

It is a fact that not everyone is going to like you. You just cannot help that. We are not all destined to be homecoming kings and queens for life.

This fear of unpopularity causes some to live in the shadows rather than step into the sunlight. They refuse to take positions on issues or to stand up for what they believe in or to speak up for themselves when they have been wronged. Bill Cosby, who has been voted the most popular entertainer in America, has said that striving for popularity can be a mistake. "I don't know what the secret of success is," he told one writer, "but here's what I know the secret of failure to be: *trying to please everybody*."

It takes courage to confront your fears, to say "This job is a dead end," "This relationship is poisonous," "This life-style is toxic." But you have to decide that, as the late civil-rights leader Fannie Lou Hamer said, you are sick and tired of being sick and tired before you can walk away and start anew.

Many people achieve far beyond their dreams, but some have difficulty reconciling their achievements with their negative self-image, with their fear of success, which can be just as debilitating as a fear of failure.

People with poor self-images feel undeserving of success and it is not unusual for them to unconsciously set about sabotaging their own success because they are ill-equipped to handle it. One of the major challenges I had to deal with was the fear of success. In Miami, I founded a community organization that was designed to empower and inspire people to become actively involved in the community and in their own lives. And it became so successful that I felt I could not handle its continued growth. I panicked, I started doubting whether I had the leadership abilities necessary to take it where it should go. So I turned it over to someone else and walked away. At that point in my life, I did not feel deserving and my lack of self-approval impeded my path to my dream.

## The Fear of Success

Just as it can be deadly to personalize your defeats, there is an equivalent danger in making too much of your victories in life. We need to maintain our balance as much with our successes as our losses, as much with the grand and good things that happen to us as with the terrible blows. Victories can become obstacles to your development if you unconsciously pause too long to savor them. Too many people interpret success as sainthood. Success does not make you a great person; how you deal with it decides that. You must not allow your victories to become ends unto themselves. Rather, think of them as the springboards to new achievements or to the next level of accomplishment.

Acknowledge your victories, but don't get overly enthralled with the applause. Instead, take a bow and then raise the stakes. Ask yourself how you attained the pinnacle and then determine what you need to improve on and where you need to go next.

On the other hand, when you are fearful of success you may become your own worst enemy. The celebrity magazines are full of examples of this. There are probably enough stories to launch a special magazine called *Self-Saboteurs Weekly*. Mike Tyson is a prime example, of course. The mentors in his life developed the fighter to the highest level but they neglected the development of the man. He won the title but Tyson never became a true champion.

Tyson was equipped to become successful but not to BE successful. He was afraid of it and his escalating pattern of self-destructive behavior proved it. In the end, his career appears to have been destroyed by his fear of success. He sabotaged it himself. As tough as he was physically, Tyson could not fight off his own self-destructive impulses. Tyson's self-destruction illustrates the importance of acquiring self-knowledge and self-approval. If your achievements exceed your level of expectation you may begin to engage in self-destructive behavior.

## Falling Stars

You need to grow emotionally as you achieve success; otherwise, you will not be able to build on it. Superstar athletes are highly visible examples of this, but it applies to all aspects of public and private life. Athletes are elevated to the status of superheroes, but too often they are not provided the psychological and emotional tools to deal with that sort of adulation. It is difficult for these successful young men and women to grasp the fact that at a time when life is handing them so many rewards, they need to understand some serious issues.

Michael Jordan, one of the most admired athletes in the world, became aware of that fact when he found himself under scrutiny because he was found to have written checks for large amounts to pay off gambling debts to individuals of questionable reputation.

Michael, who earns a reported $15 million a year for playing basketball and for product endorsements, admitted the checks were to pay off private gambling wagers with these men, whom he said he met through friends. Because the wagers were made on card games and golf matches rather than his own sport, there were no criminal charges or even criminal investigations made, but the matter loomed large in the headlines.

At first Michael said the only thing he regretted was that the matter had become public. But after pondering the situation a bit more, Michael said he had erred in judgment. Then he reflected on how his status as a superstar had affected his life. "My situation is totally outrageous," he told the *Chicago Tribune*. "People ask me to explain it and I can't. I don't know what I did to put myself in this predicament other than to be myself."

He said his public image had taken on a life of its own, "And I'm like this little machine that's got to direct it, so that it acts the way most people perceive it should act. . . . People count on you so much that you start to try to constantly maintain it, and that's when the pressure starts to mount. Suddenly, everything you do, you have to think, 'How is this going to be perceived?' "

Michael Jordan and others in his position need to be more concerned about questions of integrity than of image. They need to have this question ready when asked to take part in dubious activities: *"Does this fit with who I really am?"*

Superstar athletes such as Michael are forced to live in the public eye, under constant scrutiny, and few young people are emotionally equipped to handle that pressure, Jordan acknowledged. On the one hand, his image is that of a highly focused and mature athlete, "but on the other side of me is a twenty-nine-year-old who never really got the chance to experience his success with friends and maybe do some of the crazy things that twenty-seven-, twenty-eight-, twenty-nine-year-old people will do. And sometimes I have those urges to do those things. . . ."

Michael is blessed with a perceptive mind as well as incredible athletic gifts. Not many superstars are so fortunate. The publicity about his gambling debts surfaced within a few months of a few other minor controversies that, for the first time in his career, provided an unflattering, though hardly damning portrait of him. He handled it, he said, because he had been expecting it.

"Very few people go through their lifetimes without

scars," he told the *Chicago Tribune*. "And I went through a six- or seven-year period without them. Now I have a couple of scars, and I've got to mend them and keep moving on. The scars won't go away, but you know you're going to be a better person because of it."

Michael is learning to apply his talent and commitments not only athletically but to other areas of his life. He is developing a larger vision of himself that enables him to overcome his fears and the incredible pressures placed upon him by his superstar status.

## The Winner's Project

My company has a program called "The Winner's Project" to help successful people from all walks of life deal with the fear of success. It involves essentially six steps:

1. We create a climate in which the assets that helped a winner achieve success in his or her professional realm can be adapted to bring success in personal relations and in new professional fields.
2. We help the winner understand himself and separate that "self" from the job, the money, the public acceptance and the public scrutiny, both spiritually and emotionally.
3. We provide training in the "Four Stages of Personal Growth," that show how self-awareness, self-approval and self-commitment are essential for self-fulfillment.
4. We help winners solve shared problems and allow well-adjusted winners to form support groups to explore the individual's value as a human being rather than as a successful person.
5. We work to reconcile the individual's public image with his or her self-image.
6. We help the winner develop a larger vision and strong

self-approval in order to decrease the possibility that that person might become abusive of drugs or alcohol or otherwise sabotage himself or herself.

Much of our human potential goes unused because we do not feel deserving of the achievements we could produce if we were comfortable with ourselves. Your hunger to use your gifts to realize your dreams will give you that special drive and focused consciousness.

There was an anthropologist whose dream was to study and live among a tribe of African headhunters. He had great difficulty in developing a relationship with these isolated and highly suspicious people. His fears of them held him back. They were legitimate fears. It is wise to fear that a headhunter may take your head. He worked for years without winning acceptance until he lay in bed one night and focused on his reasons for being there among those people. And he concluded that the worst thing they could do to him was take his life. He decided his dream was worth the risk, and he began the next morning with a much bolder, a much more determined approach.

And as his boldness and confidence increased, he found that he was more accepted. He gained what he had so long been denied. When his colleagues asked him how he had overcome the cultural barriers, he replied, "When life can no longer threaten you with death, what else is there?"

There is nothing else. The majority of the fears that we have are not life-and-death fears. And yet we give them more power than they deserve and permit them to govern our lives.

If you find yourself submitting to your fears, stop and assess your situation. Have one of those inner conversations in which you ask yourself, "What is the worst thing that can happen to me here? Will it kill me? Why am I letting this dominate my thinking and my life? Am I the source of its power?"

## The Fear of Fat

I have known people who need a little jolt of fear now and then to wake them up. I'd been telling Bud for years that he needed to lose weight. His stock reply was, "I've been fat since I was a little boy. I'm big-boned."

Have you ever seen a fat skeleton? I haven't, and I don't know where this big-boned stuff comes from. At any rate, Bud became sick. I was there when the doctor told him that his eating habits were going to kill him because he was a diabetic.

The doctor told him that if he kept it up, he might go blind or become an amputee. Nothing really fazed Bud until the doctor mentioned that he might also become impotent.

Bud took that to heart. He went on a diet. He got into body-sculpting. He looks great. It is a shame that none of this occurred until he reached the age of forty-eight. Some people don't do anything about their health until they are told they have endangered it.

Fear may awaken a few thick-headed souls like Bud, but for most of us, it is a blocking instrument that keeps us from our dreams and potential. With the recession lingering across the country, many people have been fearful of losing their jobs. But the people who will come out on top are those who take the recession as an opportunity to invigorate their lives. These are the people who are masters of their own destiny, the people with the self-confidence to take charge of their own lives.

## Turning Bad Times into Good Pizza

Butch Carey of Morton, Illinois, was forty-six years old when he was laid off from his job as a steamfitter in 1982. With a family to support, he wasted little time dwelling on his fears. Instead, he set off on a dream he had long harbored. Many people harbor similar dreams, but few have the courage to act upon them. Butch decided to get into the food business.

Butch's family always liked pizza and had often talked about going into the pizza business. They didn't really think they were serious, but then, as they found out, sometimes necessity is the mother of SERIOUSNESS.

The development of Butch's Original Porkhouse Pizza was not unchallenged. Powerful competitors did what they could to impede the steamfitter's upstart operation. One nationwide pizza maker contacted Butch and said they would try to run him out of business. Nearly ten years later, Butch is still making the dough.

The company specializes in frozen pizzas sold through grocery stores. It turns out 15,000 pizzas a week sold in Illinois, Iowa and Wisconsin. Butch and his family had the courage to move beyond fear and take life on. When you develop that kind of consciousness, when you have that kind of spirit, nothing can stop you.

What would your life be like if you decided to go after what you want so strongly that it propels you past your fears? Butch Carey had the capacity to do that. You have the capacity to do that. We all do.

The value you bring to the planet is far more important than the fears that may impede you. Look to the future. Acknowledge your fears. Move past them.

## See Beyond Fear

If you have no vision of yourself in the future, then you have nothing to live for. The Bible says, "Where there is no vision, the people perish." This lack of vision permits some people to abuse themselves with drugs and alcohol, and to believe it gives them license to abuse the rest of society. They have no vision to propel them into the future or through difficult times.

Why is it that so many people prefer known hells to unknown heavens? Because they can't see themselves doing any better. They have no view beyond their grasp of the moment. I've often told the story of a soldier captured behind enemy lines. His captors told him that he had two choices. He could face the firing squad in the morning, or he could go through a door marked "Unknown Horrors."

The soldier chose the firing squad, and after he was executed, someone asked the leader of his captors what was behind the door. "Freedom," he said, "but very few people are willing to face their fear of the unknown."

Frightened people ask, "What will the future bring?" And the answer to that is that the future will bring whatever you show up with. Are you working on yourself right now? Are you developing yourself? Are you preparing for the future? The Optimists Club has it right when they say, "The future belongs to those who will prepare for it."

Don't be fearful of the future. Work on developing your talents and skills. If you strive to grow continually, you will be part of the future. If you get stuck, reach out for help. Maintain a winning spirit, regardless of any desperate circumstances. You must separate who you are from what happens to you.

I've known people, like Butch, who have lost their businesses and simply started over again with hardly a nod to defeat. And then, I had a friend who lost a business and took it personally. He saw the business failing and condemned himself as a failure.

He took that as a license never to try again. That is not the way it is. You must not internalize the results of what you produce if they are not what you want them to be. Take responsibility for what you produce, yes. Learn from it and grow from the experience and give it another try.

If your plan for life does not work, don't just give in to

your fear and sink into the La-Z-Boy. Work your way out of the slump. Life is studded with speed bumps. You will be cruising along, knocking them dead, in full synchronization—and then you'll hit the speed bumps. You miss a bus. Your paycheck bounces. Your car won't start. That's life. Maybe it is set up that way so that we learn and grow.

And remember, when you face your fear, most of the time you will discover that it was not really such a big threat after all.

[See exercises for this chapter in the Action Planner on page 257.]

# Eight

# The Young
# and the Goal-less

*If you can control a man's thinking, you do not have to worry about his action. When you determine what a man shall think you do not have to concern yourself about what he will do. If you make a man feel that he is inferior, you do not have to compel him to accept an inferior status, for he will seek it himself. If you make a man think that he is justly an outcast, you do not have to order him to the back door. He will go without being told; and if there is no back door, his very nature will demand one.*

—CARTER G. WOODSON

I was walking in the neighborhood one day with a classmate we called Brillo when some of the local tough guys who were members of the Fourteenth Street Gang yelled at me. "Hey, Les, we're gonna knock off a grocery store. You want to come along for the ride?"

I really didn't know if they were kidding or not. These were *rough* guys. They knew I was not into that sort of thing, but they kept hassling me. "*What's the matter? You chicken? You a sissy?*"

They got nowhere with me, so they laid into Brillo. He

was not a close friend of mine, just a classmate, a guy from the neighborhood. Brillo did not have a lot going for him either at home or at school. He was more vulnerable to their taunts.

After they badgered him for a while, he gave them just what they'd been looking for. "I'm no chicken," he said. "I'll go, but I won't go inside. *I'll drive.*"

He went with them. I went on to school. I didn't like being called a chicken but I cared more for how I thought about myself than for what those gang members thought of me.

I didn't look for Brillo on the way to school the next day. The morning newspapers told me where he was. The paper carried a full account of the robbery. When the robbers ran out, the store owner followed. He had a shotgun. He got a shot off into the car as it pulled away. Brillo was killed.

In many ways, I was not unlike Brillo. But I differed from him in one very significant way. My mother and Mr. Washington had helped fortify me against the pressures that led to Brillo's death. Thanks to their nurturing, I'd come to feel within myself that there were positive things in store for my life. Like most teenagers, I had my share of insecurities and fears, but I was comfortable and confident enough in myself that I resisted the gang's pressure to join them.

## The Greatness Within Us

I know—because I am an example—that when people have a sense of their self-worth, a sense that there is *greatness* within them, the payoff comes in the increased value they place on their own lives and the lives of others. People who see a future for themselves are much less likely to fall prey to drugs, alcohol, violence or crime. They are more likely to have an agenda for their lives, a mission that keeps them focused and shields them from the distractions and peer pressures that can knock others off course.

Early on, my mother, Mr. Washington and others invested me with a sense of purpose in life that served as my defense against the destructive forces that bombarded me in Overtown. Those mentors instilled in me that I was going to do something special, and that drugs, alcohol, poverty and hopelessness were not to be my life's companions.

We all need to be empowered with a sense that we have greatness within us. When we are young we are especially vulnerable to peer pressure and negative influences. Like all of us, the young need to be reminded of the value of their lives and the preciousness of their gifts and talents and the short time allotted them on this planet.

## Know Your Gifts and Share Them

People who do not know the value of their gifts are easy prey. There is a story about two children in Africa who were playing with rocks when some explorers approached them and offered them candy for the stones. The children gladly traded, only to discover later that the stones were *diamonds*.

Those young boys had a fortune in their hands and did not know it. Many of us are the same way. We have within us talents and skills and abilities, but we don't know what they are. We operate out of a limited vision of our gifts and capabilities.

If I had not been given a vision of my own greatness—my potential to be somebody in the world—I might well have suffered the same fate as Brillo, or I might still be in Overtown with many of my old friends, hanging out on street corners, bottle in a bag, life in limbo.

Like many of my schoolmates, I dreamed quietly as a

child. I had a sense of a greater world outside my immediate environment, and I had a feeling, instilled by mentors, that I could fit into that greater world. When I viewed the fine houses and opulence on display around the Venetian Causeway and Miami Beach, I did not feel shut out from them. I sensed that my time would come. The Fontainebleau Hotel was my vision of a fantasy castle, with Jackie Gleason and the June Taylor Dancers as the king's court. I dared to dream that there was a place for me in that castle. That was the critical difference between Brillo and me. That was what sent me on to school that fateful day when Brillo fell prey to the Fourteenth Street Gang.

My dream now is to do for others what my mentors did for me. I do it for the same reason that others, especially my Mama, did it for me.

My mother took on a great burden when, as a single woman working as a maid and cafeteria cook, she brought children into her home and made them her own. She told me recently that part of her motivation for adopting my brother and sister and me came from her own father. She said that her father, a farm laborer, worked hard to provide for her, and when she became an adult she wanted to do the same for children of her own. "I know how my daddy struggled," she said, "and I asked God to let me love children like my daddy had loved me."

## Selling Greatness

Each of us owes someone. We all benefit by reaching out and helping others. The things you do for yourself are gone when *you* are gone, but the things that you do for others remain as your legacy.

I think we should all do what we can to ease the way of those struggling to realize their value in the world, particularly the next generation, our legacy. I am intrigued by the concept of selling people on their own greatness with the same fervor that Madison Avenue sells them on the wondrous attributes of Nike athletic shoes, Chevy trucks and Calvin Klein jeans. What if our young people heard encouragement to dream and strive as many times a day as they are exhorted to drink Dr Pepper or to go to the land of Mickey Mouse?

I believe that the most important thing you can sell people is *a belief in themselves*. The most significant investment you can make is one in your own potential for greatness, your own capacity to make a difference in the lives of those around you. And yet there has never been a demonstrated economic interest in selling us on *ourselves*. Maybe others fail to see the tremendous payback for society in the selling of self-esteem. It is not nearly as obvious as the profits from the sale of more tangible items. But it is much more significant.

Young people must be told that they, as individuals, are more important than what they wear or drive or eat. You and I can help them see that their untapped potential is too vast to abandon, that they are still an unfolding of flesh and spirit, of mind, of hopes and fears, of joy and tears, of challenge and opportunity.

But if we adults are going to help teenagers, and if we are going to understand them, then we must first of all understand ourselves and how teenagers perceive us. If you listen to the messages that teenagers hear in their music and in the advertising geared toward them, and eavesdrop on their conversations, you can't help but hear heavy undertones of cynicism. That "Yeah, right" attitude. That "in your face" snarl at authority.

It infuriates parents and adults. But that attitude is certainly understandable if you look at what where it comes from. Adults preach about drug and alcohol abuse and safe sex, but preaching is often as far as it gets. Teenage cynicism is often born of adult hypocrisy.

While we preach, the messages sent out by the adult-dominated world say just the opposite. Adults write advertising campaigns for beer commercials. Adults make sexually explicit movies promoting promiscuity. Adults glorify violence and drug use. And then adults dare to say they are bewildered by the actions of teenagers who, in fact, are doing as adults are doing, rather than responding to what adults are only saying.

## Greatness Is As Greatness Does

You know, *the fruit does not fall far from the tree*. I've been reminded of this on several occasions recently. My son Calvin was very late one day when he came to pick me up. I was aggravated and I asked him why he was always late. He responded respectfully, but pointedly, "Dad, think about where I got that habit. Think about the number of times you've told us you would pick us up and you didn't, the number of times you said you'd be somewhere and you weren't."

He called me on it. And he was right. We discussed it and decided that we would work together to help each other improve. If adults are going to reach teenagers, we need to do it from a position of honesty. We adults need to know ourselves first. We need to check our *own* behavior against what we expect of the young people in our lives.

A few years ago, I was asked to speak to a group of young people in a Los Angeles neighborhood that had been plagued by gang violence, particularly drive-by shootings. I wanted to help the young people there, if I could. A contact person had assured me that there would be more than seven hundred young people in the audience and so I rearranged my schedule, with great difficulty, to make the meeting. And when I arrived, there were fewer than a dozen people present. Probably only seven or eight young people were on hand.

This upset me and I allowed it to affect my presentation. I had a bad attitude. I spoke AT them, and not TO them. I did not give them my best. After I spoke, I let it be known to the organizers that I was upset at the poor turnout. I felt they had misrepresented the event to me. They apologized but I was still angry when I returned to my hotel and went to bed.

At 3:00 A.M., my bedside telephone rang. It was the sponsor of the failed gathering. She was apologetic, but she said a young man who had attended my speech had come to her home and was demanding to speak with me. She said his name was Kenyatta and that his brother had been one of those killed in a drive-by shooting.

Irritated, I told her to put him on the telephone. Kenyatta let me have it right away. "Mr. Brown, when you spoke tonight, you did not give your best and I was really disappointed with you. I've heard one of your tapes in which you say, 'You must deal with circumstances such as they are. And regardless of what occurs, you must do your best. Regardless.'"

This young man had me in his sights. He was pumped up.

"Wait a minute," I replied. "They promised me at least seven hundred young people would be there."

Kenyatta was prepared to match my righteous indignation with his own outrage.

"Mr. Brown, I understand what you say, but you have said *that we must deal with circumstances just as we find them.*"

## My Personal Wake-up Call

I rolled out of bed. He was calling me out. I gave him my best argument. But he was relentless in holding his ground. And finally, I conceded that he had a legitimate point. I apologized.

"Good," he offered. "It takes a *big man* to do that."

I was irritated at first, but Kenyatta was right. And I was once again guilty of, as they say on the street, *talking the talk but not walking the walk.*

If young people are to respect us, we have to do that. It is unrealistic of us to expect them to do otherwise. To help them develop THEIR greatness, we must first evaluate our performance. Here are a few things to consider when dealing with young people, or with anyone over whom you have authority.

• *Check yourself.* Do you live what you preach or are the people around you getting conflicting messages? Are you saying, "Do as I say, not as I do"? Do YOU drink and drive? Do YOU lie to others in front of your subordinates or children? Do YOU respond to problems with temper tantrums or pity parties? Do you cheat on your taxes? Do you call in sick when you aren't? Do you hang out with negative people? If you are hypocritical, you should not be surprised if others' response to your message is cynical and disrespectful. Live your own advice.

• *Get involved in their lives.* Don't just ask about their lives, take part. Can you name your children's friends? What is your child studying right now in school? What is your child's favorite activity? When is the last time you did something *that your child wanted to do*? Take on a project together. Help find hobbies or leisure-time activities that you both enjoy. Let your children see you in all of your greatness and in all of your flaws. Let them see that you are trying your best but that you know you sometimes fall short of what they need.

• *Celebrate their greatness and their uniqueness.* Goethe said, "We can't form our children on our own concepts; we must take them and love them as God gives them to us." All young people have something special, just as all adults do. Deal with them not as unformed, uncertain adolescents but as individuals of unlimited potential, people with greatness within them. *Respect their gifts and they will come to respect themselves.*

## Lighting the Way

Yvonne Deleveaux was a few years ahead of me at Booker T. Washington High School. She was in Mr. Washington's homeroom but she was not in his drama class. She was not a strong enough student. Because he was the speech and drama instructor, Mr. Washington had a stage in his classroom. And Yvonne wanted to get on that stage badly. She pestered Mr. Washington nearly every day. Mr. Washington did not think Yvonne had acting ability but he was a great admirer of persistence in any of his students. Finally, Mr. Washington relented. Yvonne jumped onto the stage and began to dance. And she was good!

So good that Mr. Washington wrote a dance scene into a benefit show that he was directing. He chose Yvonne and a few other girls to perform in the dance scene and then he sent them to the high school's dance instructor for training. The instructor did not share Mr. Washington's elevated opinion of the girls' abilities. She sent the girls back and complained that Mr. Washington had sent her "only the dumbest girls with the biggest butts" to work with.

That attitude antagonized Mr. Washington. He believed in Yvonne and the other girls so he decided to work with them himself. He enlisted the help of a friend, and together they taught the girls a dance routine for the show. The girls began performing under his training and became so skilled that the dance instructor who had originally criticized them asked Mr. Washington if he would persuade Yvonne to perform in a state competition under her direction. Yvonne did, and she won that too.

Once she got started, Yvonne never stopped dancing. After high school, she became a performer in clubs and hotel revues around Miami and across the country. She still dances and she now shares her gift with others by working as an activity director in a nursing home.

Because Mr. Washington recognized that Yvonne had a dream and the determination to pursue it, he helped her find a purpose and a joy in her life.

## Bring Out the Best in Yourself and Others

I believe that when you bring forth the best there is within you, you lift yourself to greater and greater heights. I don't believe we have the right to sit on our greatness. We have the responsibility to put our gifts to work. I've tried to make it my business to get people to face their greatness as a way of life. It is important to let our young people know that there is importance and significance to their stories, their songs, their concerns, their questions, their ideas, their answers and their journeys. Tell them that all their best is still within them. Inspire them to reach within for it, and bring it out for the world to marvel at.

Teenagers are sometimes bedeviled by their own temperaments. Much of the time, they are as confused by their own behavior as their parents are. They need to understand that no matter what outer behavior they find themselves presenting, there is still goodness inside them. Let them know that you see it even if they don't. Beneath that coolness, that tough stance, that hard cynicism, that rebelliousness, there is still the good child, the person with goodness to share. They need to give themselves permission to unleash that goodness—not to please adults or authority figures, but in order to reflect that higher consciousness: the best of themselves.

I have a little checkup list for teenagers that can help them evaluate their lives.

• *Check yourself.* What do you want from your life? Is your behavior bringing the results you want in life? Is it moving you toward your dreams? How do you see yourself in the future? How can you get to where you want to be? Are you molding now what you want to be as an adult?

• *Check your relationships.* Do your friends tear you down or build you up? Do they weaken you and make you dependent on their approval? Or do they make you feel strong and capable? Measure the value of each relationship against how that person makes you feel about yourself. Is this person more likely to help you get on the honor roll or the detention list?

• *Get a plan.* No pressure here; it doesn't have to be for your lifetime. Just for the next week, month and year. Get some help and determine the steps you need to take to make that plan work. What is it that you like to do? How do people make a living doing that? Are you interested in making that your career? Think about the type of person you want to become, not the type of possessions you want to accumulate.

• *Recognize your own value.* Respect yourself. Think about the activities that give you the most satisfaction, the skills or talents that you have that you can build upon and turn into lifelong gifts. Develop them, take pride in your abilities and your creativity and the strength of your character. Each of us is unique; celebrate your uniqueness and the diversity of the world around you. Be secure within yourself so that no one controls your destiny but YOU.

• *Seek mentors and role models.* Sit down and talk to people who are doing what you think you want to do. Volunteer to work for them or ask to spend a week following them as they work. Role models don't have to be adults; they just have to be *positive* people.

## A Voice to Follow

I dreamed about being on the radio all the time when I was in high school. Listening to the radio one night in my bedroom, I heard a familiar voice. It was Delmar, a guy from school who was a few years older than me. I discovered that he worked as a part-time announcer at the station. "That is something I would like to do," I told myself.

When you have a dream and you recognize it as something you can actually strive to realize, I believe life opens up and offers opportunities. Delmar became my role model and mentor. I became his shadow. I would follow him around school asking him how he got his job at the station and how he liked it and what he did there.

Delmar seemed to enjoy the attention. He invited me over to the station one day and I took that as my permanent invitation to join him. I became his volunteer assistant, sharpening his pencils and ripping the Associated Press news off the wire machine so he could read the news, weather and sports.

It was actually Delmar who gave me my very first on-air opportunity. He worked weekends, so one Saturday night, when it was just the two of us at the station, he offered to let me do the midnight station break. I was so excited! I called my mother and all my relatives and friends. I told them I was going to be ON THE AIR!

When the clock struck twelve, Delmar handed me the microphone and I tucked my chin into my neck to get my radio voice out there and said, *"This is WMBM, Miami Beach!"*

I was so proud!

I called my mother up and said, "Mama, did you hear me?"

She said, "No, Leslie, it was so fast, I missed it."

"Oh," I said, "Well, don't worry, Mama, I'll be on again next week, same time, same station!"

That one spot, once a week, was *everything* to me back then, and I'll never forget how kind Delmar was in helping me work on my dreams. He was only a few years older than me, but he shared his gifts and helped me find my way.

Delmar did a rare thing, not just for a young person but for any person. He helped me celebrate MY specialness. He saw it in me and helped me bring it out.

That ability comes to people who see the greatness in themselves. They learn then to see it in others too.

## A First-Class Misjudgment

I make a habit of flying in first class on airplanes because it is a good way to meet business leaders and learn from them. The tickets are more expensive, but it can be a bargain education—unless you make the mistake of judging someone by appearance only. I got on a plane recently and my seat was next to a very elderly gentleman who was asleep when I boarded. He wore two hearing aids and his attire was very rumpled. To me, he did not appear to be a business leader. He looked more like someone's grandfather whose family had chipped in to fly him to a family reunion.

I climbed over him to my seat and went to sleep myself until the flight attendants woke us up to feed us. I spoke just briefly to him during the meal, and then pulled out some reading material because I felt he probably had difficulty hearing me. And, in truth, I thought we would not have much to talk about anyway. *This proved to be a colossal misjudgment.*

After the plane landed, I saw him struggling to get his luggage from the overhead compartment. I pulled his heavy suitcase down and carried it to the gate for him. After he thanked me and began dragging the suitcase through the terminal, a young man in a business suit, who had been on the plane, rushed forward to help him. "Can I help you, Mr. Deming?" he said. The old man said "No, thank you," picked up the suitcase and walked slowly away.

The guy in the business suit then walked up to me. "I almost came up and asked you to trade seats so I could talk to him. Do you know who that was?"

Warily, I confessed that I did not.

"That was W. Edwards Deming, the management genius who taught the Japanese how to organize their industries after World War Two," the young fellow said. "They call him 'the Messiah of Management.' The country's top executives pay thousands just to hear him speak for a few hours on how America can regain its manufacturing strength."

I can't tell you how many times I have lectured my own children and other young people that they should not judge others by appearances. I've drilled others on welcoming diversity into their neighborhoods, into their workplaces, into their schools. I tell them that just because someone looks different, it is a mistake to prejudge because we all have greatness within us, regardless of how different we may be. And now I can tell them that as a reformed first-class sinner, I know whereof I speak.

My mistake with Mr. Deming cost me an incredible opportunity to meet a man who has served as an example for thousands of business leaders around the world.

## Our Psychic Infrastructure

I have been witness to what happens when young people do not have any mentors and when they do not see any value in their lives. I've seen them fall prey to low self-esteem and allow others to control their destiny. I give seminars in jails and prisons around the country, including the Cook County Jail in Chicago, one of the toughest in the nation. There I see teenagers—many of them gang members—awaiting trial or incarcerated for murder, rape, aggravated assault, drug dealing and possession, weapons trafficking.

When I go to the Cook County Jail, I feel much like those private engineers must have felt when they were called to plug up the hole beneath the Chicago River. That hole could have been patched for as little as $10,000 early on, but because it was ignored, the damage costs have run into the hundreds of millions. The underground flooding, though apparently triggered by a construction error, drew attention to the neglected state of the physical infrastructure of our cities and our nation—our bridges and highways—the unseen essentials that keep the country running. And whenever I visit the Cook County Jail, I am left to ponder the neglected state of our nation's psychic infrastructure and the enormous unseen costs that result.

There's an alternative to treating criminals like animals with the result that they learn to act like animals. What if, while we had them incarcerated, we tried to build them into people who see their own potential value to society? What if we tried to sell them on their potential to contribute to the world, rather than condemning them and locking them out?

Instead of taking large segments of their lives away from them, what if we gave their lives back to them? What if we endeavored to give them an appreciation of their own worth? What if we gave them values and enlightened them? What would happen if we saturated our prisons and jails with messages of hope and self-appreciation rather than merely threats and punishment?

I believe we should work to make people *better* instead of *bitter*. The Reverend Martin Luther King said, "There is nothing more dangerous than to build a society with a large segment of people in that society who feel that they have no stake in it, who feel that they have nothing to lose. People who have a stake in their society protect that society but when they don't have it they unconsciously want to destroy it."

The hole in the riverbed wall in Chicago went unnoticed by most people and untended by the bureaucracy until it was too late to prevent millions in damages. The dire straits of our societal infrastructure pose an even greater threat. The costs of the neglect are evident in our overflowing prisons, our soaring crime rates, divorce rates and suicide rates, as well as in our country's great problems with homelessness, physical and sexual abuse, hate crimes and racial injustice.

The acquittal of the Los Angeles police officers involved in the beating of Rodney King, and the rioting that followed, exemplify the extent of the decay in our societal infrastructure. I heard it remarked shortly after the verdict was announced and the rioting began that it was perhaps better that the jury ruled the way it did. If the police officers had been found guilty, our society could well have patted itself on the back and swept the issue of racism back under the rug. But when the jury found the policemen not guilty, the true nature of racial relations in this country could not be denied.

Whenever I see that wrenching video of the Rodney King beating, I wonder about those policemen who stood there and did not participate. It occurs to me that they did not take part in the beating because they knew it was wrong, and yet, they did nothing to stop it. To me, they are every bit as guilty as the officers who bludgeoned Rodney King. They represent those of us who stand by and do nothing about our societal problems such as sexual bias, homelessness and racial injustice. We are just as much to blame as those directly responsible. Martin Luther King said, "Cowardice asks the question 'Is it safe?' Consensus asks the question 'Is it popular?' But *conscience* asks, 'Is it right?' "

Those police officers were sworn to uphold what was right, and they did not. They responded to either cowardice or consensus, not to their duty, not to what was right. They are symbolic of our societal decay. But we are not without hope. In the rioting that ensued, others stepped forward, answered their consciences, and did what was right at great risk both to their personal safety and to their standing in their community. I'm referring to those who came to the rescue of the truck driver who had been beaten by a rioting mob. These people were not sworn to uphold the public safety, but they took that responsibility on because they clearly saw what was called for, what was right. The beating of Rodney King was beyond any acceptable behavior for police officers and the beating of that truck driver was an act of street violence that went far beyond the anger and outrage triggered by the verdict in the King case. Both were acts of horrifying cruelty.

Those policemen who beat or did nothing to stop the beating of Rodney King, and those who beat the helpless truck driver, represent the lowest in us all. Those private citizens who assisted the truck driver represent the highest. And I have to add that Rodney King's statements during the rioting also to represent the highest in us. He had every reason to be silent and let those buildings burn as the rage must burn within him. Rodney King did not have to say a thing. He could have remained silent. Instead, he took the high road. We are all stuck here for a while, he said, "Can't we all get along?"

Rodney King, the man whom police beat like an animal, spoke to the highest that is within men and women. He called for forgiveness. If Rodney King can call for peace and harmony and cooperation, surely we can all do it.

If we are to become better as a society, we need to strive for the highest that is within us. When men sworn to protect the public can beat or stand by and watch the beating of a man, when employers have to conduct their own literacy programs in order to bring their workers to competent levels, when street gangs recruit with greater ease than colleges and job programs, when suicide rates among young people are described as "epidemic," then it is obvious that our future is flowing into a gaping hole. It is time we rebuilt our society's infrastructure.

## Building from Within

I was once asked to speak at a housing project in New Jersey, and before the event, a few city administrators drove me around to show me how they were spending millions of dollars to refurbish the subsidized housing. We went into one of the apartment buildings to speak with community leaders, and when the door to the building was opened, the stench of human filth and decayed garbage staggered me. The hallways and staircases of the building were saturated with neglect and decayed spirits.

I sat in an apartment in that building and I listened to residents and community leaders talk about what government needed to do to make their lives better, and I could only think that nothing would change really, not if millions and millions were spent refurbishing the housing project, unless an equal investment was to be made in the redevelopment of the people who lived there.

Without an investment in the people themselves, the building project was defeated before it was begun. It doesn't take a rocket scientist to realize that the most valuable thing the city officials could have done for those residents was to invest them with a sense of their own potential so that they could see the value of maintaining their own buildings and have a greater sense that they could take responsibility for their own lives and improve their own standard of living.

When people learn to appreciate themselves as having potential and when they see themselves as having a future, then they dare to dream. They establish goals and work toward them. They take responsibility for their own lives.

I believe government should lend assistance to people in need, but it has a more profound role. Government should also support programs that give people insight into methods that can empower them to take charge of their own lives. People can begin to take responsibility for their lives and pull themselves up the economic ladder only if they see that there is a future for them. I believe that it would be better to build that sense of self-worth in people than to merely build them public housing. In order to take responsibility for your own life, you have to believe in yourself and in the greatness within you. You have to believe that you have the power to seize control of your own destiny.

That is what the residents of Westlawn did. Westlawn is a neighborhood on the South Side of Chicago. In the early 1970s, a wave of gangs and crime swept into that area of the city, but the residents of Westlawn were determined that they would not surrender their quality of life to the surge in violence.

While surrounding neighborhoods became infested with decay and surrendered to it, Westlawn took charge of its own destiny. Its residents united in a manner that became a model for the city and nation. Out of thirty-three blocks in the neighborhood, twenty-two block clubs formed. Signs went up throughout the area: THE 67TH AND 68TH S. CLAREMONT BLOCK CLUB WELCOMES ONE AND ALL. NO LITTERING. NO GANGS. NO BALL PLAYING. NO LOUD MUSIC. RESPECT YOUR NEIGHBOR. DRIVE SAFELY.

Some block clubs posted their own speed-limit signs. Parents organized sports leagues to keep their children occupied in worthwhile activities. Strict rules were enforced even inside the gymnasium. A neighborhood-watch program was set up with citizens-band radio operators notifying police immediately of any suspicious activity. Graffiti "paint-overs" and alley cleanups were scheduled several times a month. Neighbors worked together to clean up and maintain their property. Some block clubs pooled funds to purchase matching streetlights for every yard. Residents swept their own street gutters each week. Westlawn stayed clean and it stayed proud. Residents nurtured their self-esteem and the payoff was a better life.

Police who work in the Westlawn neighborhood today say that the success of its residents borders on a miracle. Gangs are present throughout Chicago and even many of its suburbs, but Westlawn remains relatively free of gang influence. The residents of Westlawn still meet several times a month to discuss the status of their dream. They are living that dream. THEY TOOK LIFE ON!

## Grounded in Self-esteem

The people of Westlawn believe in their own power to live in the midst of a crime-ridden area of Chicago without letting it live within them. I believe one of the most important things people must do is stay grounded in themselves and firm in their sense of their own greatness in the face of life's challenges.

One of the most fascinating people I've met is the great performer Gladys Knight. In a profession where people easily fall prey to delusions of grandeur or the trappings of wealth or the false security of alcohol or drugs, she has endured. She is to her profession what Westlawn is to its part of the city: one who perseveres and endures; one who survives and thrives.

Gladys has been performing since she was a little girl, and though her career, like most, has had its ups and downs, she always appears to hang in there as a class act personally and professionally. Gladys drives her own children to school, she waits in line in restaurants with everyone else, she stays in touch with her family and her small circle of longtime friends.

I asked Gladys how she stays centered in her life and she said that even as a young girl, when she was on the road with other performers on the "Chitlin' Circuit" of southern nightclubs, *her upbringing never left her*. In fact, she said, she knew her family would kill her if she got mixed up in the drugs and alcohol that consumed other performers. She watched many people she admired go down in flames, but she decided that she would never follow them. She admired and emulated their artistic accomplishments, but not their self-destructive impulses.

She is a celebrity, but she does not live for celebrityhood. I was curious about how she managed to do this, and when I met her and got to know her, I discovered that Gladys perseveres because she knows exactly who she is. She allows neither the applause nor the down times to affect her as a human being. She is devoted to her family and to constantly developing her gifts. She believes in her value as a human being and she attributes this strong sense of self to the strong family values instilled in her as a child.

Gladys's example proves that we can determine our circumstances; they don't have to determine us. A lot of people yield up their individuality under peer pressure in the desire to be liked or to belong. Most of us want to be loved and to be accepted. I believe the lower your self-esteem, the more driven you are to please other people without taking into account your own needs, feelings and reputation.

That is why it is important that we empower ourselves early on with a sense of our own specialness and uniqueness, our capacity for greatness, and thus increase our sense of self-worth.

I know this, because I am an example of it. Because of Mr. Washington's liberating words, I became aware of a larger life, a greater destiny. My constant fantasy was charting my path to greatness. That is why it is so important for you to hold on to a vision of who you want to be and where you want to go. It is equally important to fashion a vision of what you want to leave behind.

If you died tomorrow, are there three things that your eulogists could say you did to make the world a better place for your having lived in it? What cause can you take on? Who can you offer a hand to? I believe that those of us who have overcome obstacles and difficulties in life derive particular pleasure in giving assistance to others. I believe people who have endured and persevered radiate a special kind of power and giving something back empowers them further. We feel we owe a debt and we go back into the places we have been to champion others.

One of the people I remember best from my own younger days is Charles L. Williams, the principal of Booker T. Washington High School. Mr. Williams was a man who had high expectations and visions of greatness for the students of Booker T. His theme for the school was *"Not the largest, but the best."* He demanded the best from his teachers and his students, and because of that, both were high-achieving.

Like Mr. Washington, who followed his lead, Mr. Williams carried himself with great dignity and anyone who acted up was regarded as an affront to both him and his beloved Booker T. High. I can hear the great ringing voice of Mr. Williams even now, reacting to a disturbance I once incited.

"Come here, SONNY BOY! How DARE YOU!"

For a principal, he could move pretty fast. Mr. Williams once chased me all the way through the girls' locker room *while they were showering* because of something he'd seen me do. He caught me too, and as he was dragging me past the cafeteria, where my mother happened to be working that day, I called out to Mama for help. She looked out the door, saw me in Mr. Williams's clutches and offered these consoling words: *"BEAT HIS BEHIND GOOD, Mr. Williams!"*

## The Slap of Authority

Between my principal and my Mama, I was bound to get straightened out sooner or later. On another occasion, I got in hot water for mimicking Mr. Williams behind his back. He had a habit of slapping his hips with his hands as a sort of body-language exclamation point. I remember him reading someone the riot act in the assembly hall one time. I was standing behind Mr. Williams and every time he slapped his hips, I slapped mine. He couldn't see who was doing it, but the students around us were cracking up.

He got wise and faked like he was going to slap his hips again. When he heard me slap mine directly behind him, he wheeled around. I thought I was dead meat. *Order the tombstone, Mama, he's gonna bury me for sure.*

But Mr. Williams didn't need a shovel. He had his tongue.

"YOUNG MAN!" he blasted, "YOU ARE SWIMMING IN A POOL OF IGNORANCE, AND YOUR MOTHER IS THE LIFEGUARD!"

I spent a long time living that one down. Mr. Williams created a no-nonsense atmosphere in his school, and whenever I go into a school now to speak I try to do the same. I refuse to be intimidated. My job is to get through to the students. That is what my commitment is and I endeavor to make that happen, no matter what.

## A Class Clown Goes Back to the Circus

I often ask to speak to special-education classes in high schools because, as you know, I was a special-education student. I conducted a series of classes for such a group at Miami Northwestern High School in my old Liberty City neighborhood, and I found it exhilarating and challenging.

On the first day of class, I walked in and the young people were having a ball! Playing music, playing cards, roughhousing. They were tearing the place up. Actually, it reminded me very much of the classroom scene on that fateful day when the principal banished me to the special-education class.

When I entered the classroom, the students paid little attention to me. I always tell the school supervisors that if students become disruptive while I am there not to take them out of class. The disruptive students are the ones who need to hear what I have to say. I want them to get the benefit of the discussion.

I tell the students that in life there are many distractions. I was once one of them. In school, I was a primary distractor, the class clown. I know what is going on with such students. They don't know who they are. They know that by causing trouble, they will at least be recognized as being alive, as existing.

When I see these young clowns, I see myself, someone who was written off as being slow or stupid or dumb and not likely to amount to much.

When I entered that chaotic classroom in Miami to speak to the special education students, I employed a technique that I have devised for such situations. Remember the old cowboy and Indian movies in which either a cowboy or an Indian pretends to be crazy so that the enemy won't mess with him? I borrow from that strategy, except that I act crazy to *get* their attention.

I stood in front of this chaotic class of special-education students, I faced the blackboard, my back to them, and I began talking to myself—gesticulating and jaw-boning like a crazy man.

As I stood up there mumbling and gesturing, the special-education students quieted. Many leaned forward in their desk chairs. *"Who is this guy?" "What is he saying?"*

This is what I was saying, inaudibly at first, and gradually louder and louder as I received their full attention: "There is GREATNESS in this room. I know it is here!"

Slowly, I turned to face them, still talking to myself, fixing them in an intense gaze one by one. "There is GREATNESS in this room! I know it is here! I can feel your vibration. Where are you? There is SOMEBODY in this room I am in TUNE with. You are not supposed to be here. You are just passing through. WHO ARE YOU?"

## Greatness Denied

I walked toward one young man on my right.
"IS IT YOU, BROTHER?"

Meekly, he said, "No, no, it's not me."

I stepped toward a young lady. Got right in her face.
"IT'S YOU!"

"No, no, no, it's not me," she said, cowering.

I spun and scanned the room intently.

"Somebody in this room has GREATNESS within them.
I can feel the vibration. Where are you? SPEAK UP!"

Finally, a little fellow in the back of the room, the puniest, meekest-looking kid in the class, stood up and said,
"HERE I AM!"

And I said, "YES, I knew that YOU would stand. But
the truth is that there is GREATNESS in EVERYONE in this
room!"

Over the following two weeks, I drilled this class on
their own greatness. I tried to create an environment of open
communication and to create a bond among them.

I told them my story, how I had been where they were,
and I told them it was important that they understand themselves and each other—especially that they share their
dreams with each other.

It is always interesting to see how the students come
together in this environment. Schools generally offer such a
passive learning experience. Students aren't encouraged to
talk about their feelings much. They are intimidated.

I've found that when you ask either children or adults
to consider who they are, what the influences on their lives
have been so far, what their wishes and their dreams are,
*they light up*.

## Studying the Life You Live

One of the things that strikes me is that we send young people through twelve years of school in which they are asked to explore the lives and the meaning of many individuals, from George Washington to Hitler, but we devote very little if any study to the meaning of their own lives, *to who they are*.

I believe that if you give young people—or adults—an enlightened sense of self, they become *self*-motivators. Their dreams match up with their sense of self and that leads to self-approval and self-commitment.

Since self-absorption is more predominant among young people than true self-knowledge, I encourage them to be kind and affirming with each other, to nurture each other. And I encourage them also to identify something they can do together for the collective good of themselves or the community, like helping senior citizens, decreasing violence in school, forming study groups. I try to give them the sense that they can make a difference by *giving* of themselves, that they can learn more about who they are by being attentive to others.

Perhaps most important, when I speak to students in special-education classes, I try to ease their unconscious self-hatred. I know now that I had a great deal of self-hatred when I was in their position in such a class. My goal is to equip them with a sense of purpose and meaning and direction by teaching them to identify and discuss their goals and to determine what kind of help they need to become the kind of people who can achieve those goals.

I try to make all the young people I speak to aware that they are molding now what they will be in the future. I want them to know that they will *fit* into the future. I believe that if a young person does not have a vision of his or her place in the future, then he or she lacks incentive to strive and grow. When people don't see how they fit they act like *mis-fits*.

I try to give young people a greater sense of themselves, and I think, with this particular class in Miami, it worked to some degree. At the end of that seminar, I entered the classroom and said, "There is GREATNESS in this room! WHERE ARE YOU?"

And the entire class rose in unison and shouted, "*HERE I AM!*"

More than anything I do, regardless of the money I receive or the possessions I gather, that response has the greatest value in my life. Know your greatness. Help others find theirs.

[See exercises for this chapter in the Action Planner on page 259.]

# Nine

## Be Positively Charged!

*This is the true joy in life, the being used for a purpose recognized by yourself as a mighty one; the being thoroughly worn out before you are thrown on the scrap heap; the being a force of nature instead of a feverish, selfish little clod of ailments and grievances complaining that the world will not devote itself to making you happy.*
—George Bernard Shaw

When I was a disc jockey in Columbus, I received a telephone call one morning from a listener named Shirley, who was extremely depressed. She had breast cancer and the prospects of her survival were not strong. She had already undergone a mastectomy, and as a result, her husband had become distant and cold. She said she was contemplating suicide.

I kept her on the telephone. I tried to talk her out of it while I was on the air, and once I was off the air, I asked her to hold on one more day.

I asked her to please meet me the following morning to go for a drive. I did not tell her where we were going, but I had a plan. I wanted to introduce her to another woman who had been calling me for years, an incredible person by the name of Audrey.

Shirley met me at the radio station the next day and we

went for a ride. During the drive, we were both very quiet. I had no idea what to say to comfort her and to keep her from ending her own life. I was hoping the answers would reveal themselves when she met Audrey.

I asked Shirley if she would mind stopping for a moment so I could check on a friend in a nursing home. She consented, and when we arrived at the nursing home, I invited her to come in with me. This was where Audrey lived.

Sixteen years earlier, at the age of thirty-seven, Audrey had been diagnosed with multiple sclerosis. She was a nurse, married with three children. The crippling disease turned her life upside down. It forced her to move into the nursing home.

Audrey was greatly incapacitated, but her spirit remained effervescent. Everybody loved her. She was considered a blessing to everyone at the home. Though I had spoken with her on the telephone frequently, I had not visited Audrey in many months, and when we entered her room, I was startled at how much worse she had become.

She was lying on her back, her knees and arms drawn up, her body clenched against the pain. She did not have the ability to brush a fly from her face. She was incapable of even blinking. Eye drops had to be administered by the nurse's aides.

Shirley and I entered the room and found Audrey in this stricken pose, but when I greeted her, Audrey's voice came back at us with a strength seemingly beyond her physical capability.

"How are you doing, Audrey?" I asked.

"I'm doing better than good and better than most," she responded. "How do you like me now?"

Shirley was shocked. I will never forget the look on her face. She had come into the room wondering why I'd brought her to this place. But the courage that spoke out from Audrey's devastated body awakened her. Tears came to her eyes, and it seemed that her own despair began to dissipate.

## An Indomitable Spirit

We had a long talk with Audrey that morning and Shirley was a different woman when we walked out of the nursing home. Her gait had quickened. Her back had straightened. Her resolve had strengthened.

It is one thing to have faith and exude happiness when all is well in your life, when your health is good, your bills are paid, your relationships are solid and your children are acting like they have good sense. But to handle misfortune and turmoil with a similar grace is an entirely different matter. We all have the capacity to deal with tragedy in our lives; it is a matter of tapping into the positive source rather than the negative.

There are negatively charged people, such as Shirley, who allow events to control their lives, and there are positively charged people, such as Audrey, who remain in control of their lives no matter what life throws at them. *You want to be positively charged.*

There are studies showing that negative people are vulnerable to certain illnesses while optimistic and positive people live longer and spend less time in the hospital. Positive people are even said to have longer-lasting relationships. Negative people have a higher divorce rate.

Good things happen to positively charged people because they look for good things even when others see only the bad. Positively charged people are both powerful and empowering. They are leaders. They are successful. They believe in themselves and their abilities, and their enthusiasm and self-confidence affect everyone around them.

Do you know someone in your place of work whom the boss regards as irreplaceable? Someone they create positions for? Someone who seems to always have the answer to a problem? That person is positively charged.

## Hold the Upper Hand

Positively charged people choose to react positively to life because they see no benefit in letting life get the upper hand. They don't assign blame or look for a cause when a problem occurs. They look for the solution. They seek understanding.

Positively charged people are not merely positive thinkers. They don't refuse to see problems, but they do refuse to let the problems control them or their emotions. They disregard the factors that they have no control over and focus on what they *can* influence.

To help yourself develop a positive charge, read this exercise. Below are situations that commonly make people anxious along with some typical negatively charged responses.

| Situation | Negatively charged attitude |
|---|---|
| Asked to do new tasks | *I don't know how* |
| On a job interview | *Why would they hire me?* |
| Meeting someone important | *I never could do what you do* |
| Making a speech | *What do I have to say?* |
| Asking for a raise | *I need more money* |
| Starting a new project | *I will never be done* |
| Meeting an attractive person | *Looks out of my league* |

Since negative inner conversations only restrict your growth, you have to convert to a positive charge to get where you want to go. Negative self-talk is a difficult habit to break. For each of the situations above here is a positively charged response:

| Situation | Positively charged response |
|---|---|
| Asked to perform new tasks | *I'd love to learn this* |
| On a job interview | *You need my skills* |

| | |
|---|---|
| Meeting someone important | *I want to learn how you do it* |
| Making a speech | *I have a worthy message* |
| Asking for a raise | *I am worth more money* |
| Starting a new project | *This is a good challenge* |
| Meeting an attractive person | *To know me is to love me* |

## No Ifs, Ands or Buts

The difference in language and attitude is obvious, isn't it? Negatively charged people sit on their "buts." Monitor your language. Listen to the way you respond to questions and situations. Make a conscious effort to develop a positive charge. You will find that people respond more eagerly to you.

I hitched a ride with a friend the other day and as soon as we got into the car, she launched into a negative conversation about how much she hated her job. She despises it. I know. She told me and told me and told me.

Do you know people who tell you their whole life story even if you don't ask? Well, she was giving me a ride, and I couldn't very well tell her to be quiet in her own car. So I listened.

She went on and on about this job and how bad it was, and finally I interrupted. "If it's that stressful and if it is causing you that much pain, why don't you just quit and do something else?" She replied by saying something that put her in the chorus line with a lot of other people going nowhere in their lives. "I would, but . . ."

Sound familiar? It did to me, so I began testing a theory on other people. I went around for several days asking people what they were doing for a living and if it was their passion in life to do that. If they said their work was not their passion,

I asked what their real passion was and why they were not doing it. Invariably, they would reply, "Oh, I would, *but . . .*"

The "buts" just kept coming up. Sometimes it was one of but's cousins: "woulda," "coulda," "shoulda" or *"One day I'm gonna."* How many times have you heard one of those words or phrases used as an excuse? How many times have you heard them come out of your own mouth?

Too often, we repeat negatively charged words as if we are in a trance, and, in a sense, when we use them we are sleepwalking through life. We seem to be instinctively adept at finding excuses for canceling our own dreams. I think "but" and all of his family are dream killers. I think many of us would accomplish more in our lives if we put "but" and his family to rest and plunged into life.

Authors John-Roger and Peter McWilliams wrote: " 'But' is an argument for our limitations. And when we argue for our limitations, we get to keep them." "But" is a crutch; it is an excuse for procrastinators and those of us who lack the courage to live our dreams. It allows us to validate our inaction. When hard times hit, we need to look for reasons to move forward, not for reasons to idle through life.

When you don't move on life, life moves on you. It is important for you to learn to monitor your language because by listening to yourself and changing your language, you can change your attitude from negative to positive. Try these exercises if you feel you need to become more positively charged.

• Become a human Geiger counter tuned to negative language. Listen for the "buts," "couldas" and "gonnas" in your own conversations and those of people around you. Zap those negatively charged words and phrases from your own vocabulary.

• Create scenarios in which you may have reacted negatively in the past and envision yourself responding in the future with a positive charge. For example: Your boss hands back a report saying it is unsatisfactory and telling you to redo it. In the past you might have made excuses and blamed co-workers or conditions. Now you respond by thanking the boss for the opportunity to improve it.

• Consider a problem or difficult situation in your life. Is it something that you can change? Or is it something you have no control of? Positively charged people learn to attack those problems that they can change and to live with those that they cannot—thereby robbing the problem of its power over them. *If you cannot change the problem, change the way you view it.* Example: My employer is going to lay me off for three weeks. Positive response: I can spend the time seriously looking for a better, more secure job.

• Test that positive charge. For one week, concentrate on responding in a positive manner to all people and every situation. Emulate positively charged people you know. Do not criticize. Do not judge. Do not compound any problems. Encourage. Lead by example. Look for solutions. Take life on with a positive attitude.

## Good Things Happen to Positive People

You should get up in the morning and feel you are blessed and highly favored just to be alive. If you believe you are worthy of good things, you develop a sense of entitlement. A friend of mine, a journalist, landed a great assignment one day, and one of his editors remarked that it was strange how things always seemed to bounce this guy's way. "Well, sometimes good things happen to good people," he told the editor.

He was joking, but that really is how he approaches life. And life responds in kind. Several years ago, he was fired unexpectedly from a mid-sized newspaper. He found himself on the street with only a couple of months' severance pay. He was stunned.

He spent a day or two staring into the trees beyond his back porch and then he went to work. He went to the library and checked out a book with the names and addresses of editors at other newspapers around the country. He decided that he did not want to go backward in his career even though he'd gotten a good shove in that direction, so he aimed only for newspapers bigger and more respected than the one he had been fired from.

He photocopied examples of his work and his résumé and sent out a barrage of letters every day for a week. He didn't wait for responses. He called the people he had sent his applications to and he even flew at his own expense to visit a few of them uninvited. Responses trickled in. Some were curt and gave no hope. Others were encouraging but held out no job opportunities.

In the third week of his unemployment, a friend tracked him down. Several months earlier, he had helped this woman and her husband move from their apartment to a new home. The woman, an editor for an exclusive magazine geared to the ultra-rich, had offered to return the favor by giving the journalist a good free-lance assignment some day.

She surprised him by calling to tell him that she had come up with that free-lance assignment.

"I want you to go to Switzerland and live like a millionaire for two weeks," the woman said. "You can fly first class, stay in four-star hotels, and eat in four-star restaurants. We will pay all of your expenses and $2,300 for the story on how to live like a millionaire in Switzerland."

*"As luck would have it, I'm available,"* he said.

And as he was packing for the trip to Switzerland, which would find him in the Matterhorn's ski-lift line when he thought he would be in the unemployment line, he received a letter containing a job offer from one of the best newspapers in the country. He started work there, at better pay, the day after he completed his free-lance assignment on Switzerland. Instead of a pity party, he staged a *victory* party.

## Plug into the Positive Current

We all have the power to choose whether we are going to tap into the negative lower self, or the higher positive self. If sometimes you feel you need to give yourself to resentment, guilt and anger, that is understandable. But if you want to be free of those dark emotions, to rise up and move on, you can do that too.

One of my favorite positively charged people is the jazz singer Jean Carne of Atlanta. Jean co-wrote lyrics for a song she sings called "Infant Eyes." Jean is a nurturing person whom everyone likes to be around. Her song embodies her positively charged approach to life. She dedicated the song to her firstborn child, and in it she says, ". . . being strong is the one thing in the whole world that will save you." If you tap into that positive strength, you can overcome anything life throws at you, but if you take a negative charge, you let life have its way with you.

I am always amazed at people who react to hardships in their lives by saying, "How can this happen to ME?" Who would they suggest it happen to? Their neighbors? The guy who delivers their mail? Their in-laws?

Many of us act as if we were born with the great expectation that life was going to be easy. Well, if someone told you life was going to be one smooth, easy ride, I've got a special announcement: *THEY LIED!*

Sooner or later in this life, the Messenger of Misery is going to knock on your door. If he isn't at your door right now, he is probably around the corner or just up the street. Be prepared. It is going to happen. And by expecting life to give you a knock now and then, you can handle it as one of life's natural processes. There is no need to panic, to whine or to look for blame. Know that it will come and be prepared to handle it without personalizing it.

Positively charged people are capable of enduring even life's most difficult challenges. Associated Press correspondent Terry Anderson was held hostage for nearly seven years by Shiite Muslims who kept him chained, handcuffed and blindfolded much of the time. Anderson, an ex-marine, was kicked and beaten and tortured. "Often I objected, loudly and vehemently. Sometimes it worked; more often it just brought more punishment. The only real defense was to remember that no one could take away my self-respect and dignity—only I could do that," he wrote afterward.

That attitude reminds me of the small boy who was being beaten up in the back of a school bus by a bully. The bully knocked him down and the boy jumped back up. The bully knocked him down again. The boy jumped back up. Finally, the bully knocked the boy down and got on top of him, holding him there. The boy struggled but he could not move the bully. Instead, he yelled out, *"You may be holding me down, but I am standing up inside myself!"*

## Compounding a Loss

The rewards of such a positively charged attitude are great, just as the effects of a negatively charged outlook can be disastrous. I have witnessed both approaches. When I was a state representative in Ohio, I often encountered a bizarre but tragic character who frequented the streets near the statehouse in Columbus.

He was known as "Chicken Man" because he drove a station wagon with a chicken toy on top. He often had chicken feathers hanging from his clothes and he sometimes pushed a baby carriage with two little baby dolls in it. People would call out to him, tease him as "Chicken Man," and he would make funny chicken noises as he drove or paced around the grounds of state government.

One day I met someone who knew the background of this local character, and my amusement at his strange ways turned to sympathy for his tortured history.

This man had awakened one night to find his house in flames. He panicked and ran outside, and only then did he hear the cries of his two daughters who remained trapped inside. He tried to get back into the house but the flames and smoke turned him away. He made several attempts, trying different windows and doors. But he could not save them.

The fire was still out of control when a relative of the family arrived, an uncle to the girls. He ran up and asked their father where they were and when he learned that the father had saved himself but not his daughters, the uncle began to berate and beat him.

"You coward. You chicken. You chicken," he screamed.

The father did not fight back. He accepted the beating. When the neighbors pulled the enraged uncle off him, the father did not speak. He made only weak clucking sounds. That was the only sound anyone heard from him after that.

The baby dolls that he pushed around town in a small carriage were symbolic of his daughters. The strange appearance and behavior that he adopted were symbols of his anguish and his acceptance of the role of coward, a role assigned to him by someone else.

What happened to this family is a tragedy, and not only because of the young lives consumed by the flames. The father of those girls was lost, too, and that loss was just as unnecessary as the others.

I believe that the human spirit has the capacity to overcome even something as devastating as the loss of two children. That father still had gifts to share with the world. Instead of becoming a tragic waste of a man, he might have become a mentor to other children, giving them the love and direction that he could no longer provide for his departed children. He might have worked with burn victims or with the displaced or the poor.

## Let What Is Past Pass

You can't reverse the past, but there ARE things you can provide for the future. When that father gave up on life because of something in the past, he lost, and the world lost.

Candy Lightner may be the ultimate example of someone who turned a personal tragedy into a positive force for the good of an entire country. Her thirteen-year-old daughter, Cari, was hit from behind by a drunken driver and killed in 1980. The mother's anguish turned to outrage when her daughter's killer was sentenced to only two years in prison.

Mrs. Lightner said she encountered a legal system in which drunken driving seemed to be "an accepted form of homicide." She didn't react by turning inward and wasting her life. Instead, she took positive action and realized a larger vision. She organized Mothers Against Drunk Drivers and forced state after state to enact tougher laws raising the drinking age and toughening the penalties for drunken driving.

Within five years, there were 350 chapters of MADD around the country and a similar organization for students, SADD, had chapters in high schools nationwide. These organizations monitor court cases, provide victim assistance, and hold nonalcoholic activities for young people, among other positive influences.

Candy Lightner's strength of purpose has undoubtedly saved hundreds of lives and spared hundreds of parents the anguish that she went through when her own daughter was killed. She cleared away the crippling emotions and realized a far greater vision and a far more fulfilling life.

Many people perceive difficult times as a signal to stop living. Instead, take the positively charged view that difficult times are a time to *grow*. Author and abolitionist Harriet Beecher Stowe subscribed to this philosophy: "When you get into a tight place and everything goes against you until it seems that you cannot hold for a minute longer, never give up then, for that is just the place and time for the tide to turn."

There is a gospel song that says, "Lord, help me to hold

out until my change comes." The challenge is to hold on in bad times. If you hold on tenaciously, I believe, the universe is on your side. When you know within yourself that sooner or later the wheel is going to turn your way, that somehow you will endure and persevere, then you have positioned yourself to grow and succeed.

## Life Is an Adventure

Robert Elliott, who was head of the cardiology department at the University of Nebraska, suffered a massive heart attack a few years ago and was forced to spend three months looking at life from a different perspective.

While bedridden, he reflected on his near death and on his remaining time. With no history of heart disease in his family, he realized that his heart attack was primarily the result of his stressful approach to life. He wrote of his thoughts later, and offered two rules to live by:

"Rule number one: Don't sweat the small stuff.

"Rule number two: *It is all small stuff.*"

I have a similar philosophy. After intensive study and contemplation, I have reached this conclusion: "YOU CAN'T GET OUT OF LIFE ALIVE!" So why not enjoy it to the utmost? You can die in the bleachers or you can die on the field, so you might as well get out on the field of life and have a good time! Enjoy the grand adventure. Make it the most positively charged experience possible.

As long as you are here, find ways to make yourself happy. Keep in mind that this is a joyous course you have set upon. Revel in your pursuit of the dream. Savor your successes along the way. Your commitment to happiness is critical to your success. You don't need to force a smile but it helps to bring happiness to others as you go.

My high school principal, Charles L. Williams, told us,

*"Love and happiness are perfumes that you can't sprinkle on others without getting a few drops on yourself."*

I have a few sayings that I use when I need a positive charge. You are welcome to use them, too:

• *Good things are supposed to happen to me. No matter how bad it is or how bad it gets, I'm going to make it.*

• *I'm doing better than good and better than most and sometimes even better than that. I'm great and getting better.*

• *I embrace faith. I embrace peace of mind. I embrace good relationships. I embrace good health. I embrace love. I embrace every good thing in the universe.*

## Negate the Negatives

I've known people who handle difficult times by becoming extremely negative and down. Some people never take on life because they are too busy blaming and complaining about every one and everything that supposedly blocks their way.

When I encounter a moaner and a groaner, I am reminded of the story of the dog sitting on a porch moaning and groaning. A man walking by asked the people on the porch why the dog was acting this way.

"Because he's lying on a nail," one of them replied.

"Well, why doesn't he get off?" inquired the man.

"Because it's not hurting bad enough."

No doubt you have encountered people like that. When people moan and groan, "I'm sick of this job," tell them, "I'm sick of YOU."

They need to get to the point where they are sick and tired of being sick and tired. They seem to have enough energy to complain about it, which they equate with doing something about it. You are born with the power to make a difference on this planet, but you must consciously activate that power.

Some of us tend to operate out of the "victim mentality." We pretend to be far more miserable than we really are. We become volunteer victims—we volunteer for a life sentence of misery. This is a devious method of evading our greatness. It is laziness. And craziness.

There was once a study conducted on three thousand high achievers from around the world and the common denominator was not a sky-high intelligence. The study concluded that 85 percent of them had achieved their goals in life because of their attitude, and 15 percent of them because of their aptitude.

Examine your attitude right now. Are you a defeatist? A moaner and a groaner? Is that a chip on your shoulder? Do you always have a story ready on how life has done you wrong? Does your competition always win because they cheated, because they had an unfair advantage, because they were willing to take the low road?

## Toxic People

I have discovered that even a 100,000-watt positive charge does you little good if you surround yourself with a million watts of negativity. It is time, then, that you, too, become aware of the dreaded and deadly dealers of negativity, the *Toxic People*!

There are two types of people in your life. Those who nourish you, and those who drain you. Those who help you grow, and those who are *toxic* to your growth.

Toxic, draining people can drag down even the most determined positive person, and cause you to fall short of your potential. I believe that there are some people whose sole mission in life is misery-mongering. They drive little toxic green vans around the neighborhoods of positive people and create problems. They will do anything to disrupt your journey to fulfillment. They argue. They criticize. They see only the negatives in any situation. Wherever they go, this green cloud of gloom follows. It seems that dispensing despair is their destiny.

I once got a telephone call from one of them at 2:00 A.M. I'd met Sasha in Chicago a few years before, and she called me that morning to tell me she had just seen me on television. At first, she disguised her true purpose.

"Les Brown, I am so proud of you," she began. "I heard you say on that show how you and your brother were adopted and how you worked so that you could buy your mother a home. . . . But let me tell you something. I saw that picture on the program of you and your brother as babies and, well, your mother was certainly a good woman to raise you up because you all were some UGLY children. You all had some FUNNY little bald heads, you all were so UGLY! Could you have the television station take those pictures off your program? If I were you I wouldn't let nobody see those pictures. . . ."

You know, I did not ask for that telephone call at two o'clock in the morning. She called me at that hour to tease me about being a homely child. Hey, I GREW OUT OF IT! Okay?

These energy-draining people can drive your blood pressure up. They are good for neither your health nor your disposition. There is no reason to linger around anyone who brings out the worst in you. Flee from them. Cast them out. Don't try to change them; change yourself, change friends.

## Bad Relationships Drain Your Positive Charge

Seek out those who empower you, who inspire and complement you, the people who enable you to see great possibilities for yourself. It takes an enormous amount of energy to reach your goals and to strive continuously for greatness. You really cannot afford to have relationships with people whose very presence drains energy from you.

Awhile back I contacted Martha, a friend of mine who had often helped me in my work. Her talent for writing and communicating was of great help to me. But when I called her for help this time, she said she really didn't think she could be of much assistance. I said of course she would be a great help.

For years I have had to coax Martha and reassure her. Her husband was the problem. He did not see it for her. He did not encourage her in her career. He did not show her that he believed in her abilities. Such a nonaffirming relationship can be devastating. People who cannot see it for themelves usually cannot see it for you.

I believe that right now you don't even *know* 95 percent of the people who will help you reach your dream. They are strangers. Some people close to you won't help you BECAUSE they know you. They can't make the mental leap from where you have been and where you are *to where you want to go*. Don't get upset about that. Look for someone who thinks like you, someone to help you move to the next level of achievement. Don't get involved in relationships that undermine rather than support you in your search for goals. Don't let someone else's lack of vision restrict your growth.

## The Brother from Another Planet

Let me tell you about my fraternal twin, Wesley. He and I fought ferociously as children and we did a pretty good job of maintaining that relationship as adults, until recently.

We went separate ways after high school and had only occasional contact for many years. He went into the U.S.

Army and became a paratrooper. My brother is a blunt and honest man. Sometimes brutally blunt and honest. He is also something of a dreambuster. When I first embarked on my career as a professional speaker, Wesley found occasion to practice his bluntness and his honesty whenever we got together.

"What are you doing now on your dream?" he would ask.

"Oh, this is going to be my year, Wesley," I would say.

"I think we've heard THAT before," my twin would reply.

"Well, this year is different."

"Haven't we heard that before, too?"

"Yes, Wesley."

"Why don't you get a real job rather than beating your gums together?" he would ask.

At this point, the room turned red. The smoke rolled out my ears, my nose too. "Mama, make him leave me alone."

"Yeah, MIS-TER MO-TI-VA-TOR," Wesley would say, turning up the heat. "Look how much weight he's lost, Mama. He says he's FASTING. Ha! He's starving!"

Well, Wesley retired recently after twenty-six years in the army and he came to visit me for the first time at my office in Detroit. My office is in a grand old landmark building and it is really quite a wonderful and lively place. One of my staff members met Wesley at the airport and brought him to the lobby of my building.

"Is this an important building in Detroit?" my twin inquired.

"Yes," my staffer assured him.

They rode the elevator up to the twenty-first floor and when the doors opened on to my office door with LES BROWN UNLIMITED on it, Wes's eyes got bigger, my assistant said.

He came through the reception room and into my office and he shook my hand. "Les, I'm proud of you, my brother. You have really done it. I really love you," he said to my surprise.

And then he added, "And I'll really love you even more when you send me some MONEY!"

I told you he was honest. I have learned to love him anyhow. In spite of himself.

## Establish a Home-Court Advantage

Fortunately for me, along with having a dreambuster for a brother, I had my Mama and Mr. Leroy Washington, my high-school speech teacher, on my side. Mr. Washington not only set me on a new course in life but he also did me the honor of becoming my mentor and friend for life. He nourished me. He invited me into his speech classes as a participant rather than just an observer. He coached me for roles in plays; he coached me for life.

He and my mother were my home-court advantage similar to the edge that athletic teams enjoy when they are playing for a home crowd. When I played, they cheered for me, they gave me an edge in life. Find an ally, a supporter who believes in you as much as you do. Give yourself a home-court advantage.

It is not always as easy as you might think to discern which friends are supportive and which are negative and toxic. I conduct seminars with prison inmates and also with teenagers, and from my experiences with both groups I have come to the conclusion that the person who will induce your children to use drugs or commit a crime is not some stranger lurking in the shadows.

Our children are most vulnerable to people they trust and want to be accepted by.

When I ask young men and women inmates whom they were with when they first experimented with drugs or first committed a crime, they inevitably say, *I was with a friend.*

These friends are toxic: "*Hey, I thought you were hip. You scared? C'mon, give it a try, catch a buzz.*" And so are those who tell you that you are a fool to follow your dreams. So are the ones who drag you down with their gloom and doom.

Just as it is important for you to regularly examine your life and reassess your progress toward your goals, it is essential that you continually evaluate your relationships.

Now and then you need to write down the names of the people in your life and ask yourself, Is this relationship giving me what I want? Is this one good for me? What kind of person am I becoming because of this friendship?

## Seek Out Quality People

It is important to align yourself with what I call OQP—*Only Quality People*. You should endeavor to surround yourself only with people who will enrich and empower you, people who will enable you to transcend yourself and to grow. This sort of support group, your pit crew for progress in your life, can strengthen you in moments of weakness and bring you up when you are down.

Surround yourself with people who share your vision and who also are willing to support you in pursuing that vision. You cannot make it alone in this journey. If you find relationships that are not mutually constructive, if someone brings you down rather than challenges and elevates you, then you must make a decision. Can you transform this into a healthy relationship or do you need to sever it?

That does not mean of course that all of the people around you should be your yes-men. You will never grow if you are surrounded by backslapping sycophants. Although I hate being criticized by friends, I do have some trusted critics. These are people who tell me the things I need to hear. I trust their judgment, I trust their vision of me. They challenge me and make me stretch mentally and intellectually, personally and spiritually.

I get feedback from them that I would not get anywhere else and even though it doesn't always feel good to hear their criticisms and challenges, I know they care about me and about my growth. So I listen and learn.

We all need someone to coach us now and then. We cannot grow in a vacuum. We have to be willing to seek out those with wisdom and say, "I don't know what to do; help me." The fighter and philosopher, "Smokin' Joe" Frazier, said, "All of us are like the blind man at some point in our lives, standing on the corner, waiting for someone to lead us across."

You are not joined at the hip with your friends. Be prepared to acknowledge when a relationship has soured and to go your separate way. It does not have to be an angry parting. Just say, "Look here, we are growing in different directions. Our values have changed. Our goals and objectives are different now. Maybe we need to shake hands and say good-bye." Being able to break away from toxic friendships can make the difference between living your dreams or living a nightmare.

I went to school with two talented athletes, Big Cov and Larry Little. Both of them were very large, muscular fellows. Big Cov was the more gifted and naturally talented. He was larger, faster and more agile. Little, however, was more focused and more driven to succeed.

I can still see Little in my mind, running laps around Dixie Park in Overtown. He wanted to be a professional football player. He viewed it as his destiny. He had a sense of mission.

Big Cov, who could kick, tackle and play the line equally well, did not have the same discipline as Little, nor did he have the same wisdom in selecting his friends. Big Cov ran with guys whose idea of sport was stealing cars and taking them for joyrides.

These guys would taunt Little when he ran around Dixie

Park. They teased him because he was not a particularly fast runner. Little did not seem to mind the teasing. He remained focused on his purpose.

Larry Little and Big Cov were both football stars in my high school, at least they were until the police came and got Big Cov for car theft. He went off to prison. Little went off to college on an athletic scholarship. And after college, Little eventually joined the Miami Dolphins and became an All-Pro offensive guard.

I lost contact with Big Cov until I arrived at a prison in Florida to give a speech. One of the guards informed me that an inmate was claiming to be an acquaintance of mine. And sure enough, there was Big Cov. He came up from his kitchen detail, as gregarious and physically imposing as ever. He had spent the best of his years in prison. He did not die in prison; he died in an argument—shot and killed on the streets of Liberty City, not far from where he had grown up.

Two men, both talented, but the more talented of the two never honored his gifts. Big Cov never shook the toxic influences on his life; he succumbed to them, and his greatness was wasted like spilled wine.

The poet Thomas Gray wrote, "Full many a flower is born to blush unseen, and waste its sweetness on the desert air." The world never viewed the talents of Big Cov because he chose to exist among toxic people who stunted his powers. He was really not a bad guy, but he ran with the wrong crowd. *And they ran him to death.*

## Positive Friends Are Good Politics

Positive friends, on the other hand, can pull you out of trouble and take you to another level of achievement. After I was fired from my broadcasting job in Columbus, Ohio, I talked with friends and asked their help in trying to develop a strategy for my life. One friend said that since I had become a community figure through my radio broadcasts, I might consider running for political office.

I said, "What do I know about the legislative process?"

And he replied, "Most people don't know anything about the process. But you know more than most politicians about the issues that matter to people. So why not run?"

I cared about the community. I was willing to learn how the legislative process worked. I enjoyed the prospect of stretching and growing. So I went down the day before the filing deadline and registered as a candidate for state representative. And then I began researching the issues, the legislative process and political campaigning. When you challenge yourself, you discover abilities that you never dreamed you might have.

I discovered that broadcasting was a wonderful springboard for a political career. I already had name recognition, I was a good talker, and I already had a slogan. I adapted my radio motto for the campaign.

My radio sign-off had been, "Stand up for what you believe in, because you can fall for anything." And when I went around to meet people and campaign, I told them, "Tell everybody that Les Brown is still standing!"

To stir up support for my campaign, my backers and I organized a huge voter-registration drive. I went door-to-door and I went where there weren't any doors. After I'd leave someone's porch, they'd call their friends and say, *"Child, Les Brown was just at my house! You know him. The one with the big mouth that used to be on the radio!"*

None of the political experts believed I could win. I had no college education, no political experience. My opponent had been in office practically since birth. He was endorsed by the Democratic party, the AFL-CIO and both newspapers.

But *I* believed I could win. I said "I'm going on *anyhow*." When it came close to election time, a group of community leaders who I thought were going to support me came out and endorsed my opponent. That shocked me! They didn't have to do ANYTHING. They could have just stayed out of it. They blindsided me!

That is going to happen to you too when you pursue your dream. There are people out there who seem to think it is their life's mission to stop you from getting your dream. You can't let them bother you. You have to stay focused on getting ahead rather than getting even.

I kept on doing what I had to do. My opponent had thousands of dollars in his campaign chest to buy advertising. I had $735. I didn't worry about it. I kept myself positively charged and tried to stick with what I *could* do rather than worrying about what I *could not* do. With only four or five days left in the campaign, I found a quiet place and tried to think about what I might do. When you do that, the ideas come.

## The Mrs. Mamie Brown Factor

I got to thinking that when I'd been on the radio there, I'd talked a lot about my mother. And so it occurred to me to call my mother to be in my campaign commercial. *I was fairly certain that Mama had not endorsed my OPPONENT.*

And so, Mama did my commercial. I taped the commercial while talking to her on the telephone and I had Aretha Franklin singing "Holy, Holy, Holy . . . Come together people" in the background on a record.

IT WAS GREAT! In the commercial, Mama came on the air and said, *"Hello, this is Mrs. Mamie Brown. When I raised my sons I raised them to be good children. When they got out of hand, I beat their behinds and made them go right. Please vote for my son. He's a GOOD boy!"*

After the commercial hit the airwaves, my opponent called me and jokingly conceded, "Les, it's all over, you put your Mama on me!"

And do you know what? In a normal primary election in Columbus, voter turnout is very small. There was a *tremendous* turnout in my district in that election and in the general election! And most of them voted for me because my Mama said I was a *GOOD* boy!

I won!

*Thank you, Mama.* I POSITIVELY love you.

[See exercises for this chapter in the Action Planner on page 266.]

# Ten

## It's Possible!

*We grow through our dreams. All great men and women are dreamers. Some, however, allow their dreams to die. You should nurse your dreams and protect them through bad times and tough times to the sunshine and light which always come.*

—WOODROW WILSON

I've already made mention of my boyhood dream of having a fine house. As I grew older, that dream became a dream not for me but for my mother. I wanted to buy a house for her. Having been such a burden to her in my younger days, I saw this goal as my opportunity to give something back to her. I had seen fine places owned by friends so I knew it was possible to have such a house, and that possibility drove me to save my money and to look for a house in a neighborhood where Mama would be safe and proud to live.

I left the Ohio legislature because my mother had fallen ill and I wanted to make sure she received the proper medical attention. Once I'd relocated in Miami to be near her, I went to work establishing a city-funded youth-training program in my old neighborhood. With my salary from that and some money I'd saved, I scraped together $12,000 for a down payment on a nice house for Mama. Proudly, I took her to it and said, "Mama, this is for you."

I was so proud of myself. I felt that my mother could finally see that all of her love and caring and discipline had paid off. Her most troublesome son had finally amounted to something. And I'd reached a longtime goal of giving my mother a nice house. *I was living my dream!*

But as it turned out, I had moved into my dream prematurely. At the real-estate closing on my mother's new house, my lawyer asked if I'd hired someone to do a title search. New to this real-estate business, I didn't know what a title search was. "It is done to make sure there are no liens against the property," my lawyer said.

The man I was buying the house from was sitting there when my lawyer raised the lien question. He assured me there were no liens. My lawyer said she could not advise me to sign a contract on the house until a title search was completed. "Mr. Brown, I have nothing against this man, but this is the way to do business," my lawyer said.

The seller became agitated. He said he'd agreed to sell the house to me at a lower cost primarily because I was buying it for my mother. He said he'd had better offers since mine, but he had turned them down. He did not want to wait for a title search to be done. He had already lost money; he did not intend to lose time too, he said.

I was *so* close to this dream, I went against my lawyer's advice. "I believe him," I said. I signed the contract and, a few days later, I moved my mother into the house. I was so proud. As we moved my mother out of her old house, I looked with a "So THERE!" attitude at the neighbors who had always bad-mouthed me.

But two months later, I wondered if they'd been right about me after all. The mailman, impersonating a messenger of misery, brought me a legal notice in the mail from the county sheriff's office. It seems there WERE liens on the house. Huge liens. *Twenty-five thousand dollars in liens.* The seller had lied to me. My lawyer had been right. Desperately, I called the bank and tried to work out a deal to get rid of the liens, but the bankers said I had to come up with the money in six weeks or the house would be sold in an auction.

## A Hard Knock at the Door

In a matter of a few weeks, I went from high-fiving myself to high anxiety. I'd already put every penny I had toward making the down payment on Mama's new house. The well was dry. For the next six weeks, I worried and fretted. I lost twenty-three pounds. The bank put an ad in the paper announcing the auction, so I had to put a sign up in the yard, telling those who came to look at the house that the ad in the paper was mistaken: *THIS HOUSE IS NOT FOR SALE!*

But it *was*. I could not come up with the money. I was absolutely demoralized. It came down to within a day of the scheduled auction on the courthouse steps and I knew the moment of truth had come. I knew I had to tell my mother. I paced the floor all night long, wondering why this had to happen to me. *"I'm trying to do the right thing by my Mama. I'm not out robbing and stealing. Why this? Lord, why me?"*

It was a *small* pity party, but a pity party nonetheless. I took a wallop from life. I lost the house. I lost my $12,000. I lost my composure. On the day I moved my Mama out and back into her old house with the neighbors all watching and nodding their heads knowingly, I wept. I was humiliated. I was embarrassed. The neighbors were delighted.

They all stood in front of their houses and said, "Isn't that Mamie coming back? What happened to her son, *Mr. Bigshot?*"

Even as we moved Mama back in, I was *still* asking why. *"God, why would you do this to me? I'm trying to take care of my Mama and do the right thing. Why? Why?"* I broke all the rules. I began to beat up on myself. I let the problem get to me instead of me getting to the problem. I sprayed blame in all directions.

I felt so stupid and so incompetent. I had not had the simple intelligence to read the fine print. I hadn't done my homework. I began to believe the things that people had said about me in the past. I *must* be stupid. Maybe I was mentally deficient after all.

My mother came up to me while I had my head down on the back of the mover's truck crying, and she said, "*Lift your head up, boy!* You have nothing to be ashamed of. You did your best."

I said, "But oh, Mama, I am *so* ashamed. You liked that house *so much.*"

And then she stunned me. "Leslie, I never did like that house. It hurt my arthritis in my knees to walk up those stairs. I just said I liked it because you got it for me. I like my old house better."

My Mama never stops teaching me about life. I learned from that experience. And I recovered. I had to give a lecture later that week on the topic of forgiveness and I can't lecture on something unless I am living it. *I forgave the person who ripped me off, but more important, I forgave myself.* I had to get on with my life.

I realized that house was not the last house on Earth. I realized that I could have had a heart attack over a house my mother *didn't even like!* As it was, I lost everything but my spirit and the love and respect of my mother and children. So I hadn't lost all that much. Sure, people talked about me. Sure, I felt humiliated and embarrassed for a while. But I got over it. I didn't wallow in it any longer.

Instead, I came out of it determined to find my Mama a bigger and better house, a house where she wouldn't have to climb the stairs. I intensified my efforts by working harder, putting in longer hours at outside work and once again scraping together as much money as I could.

And later, I bought my Mama another house. An even

better house in a neighborhood she liked, a house where my Mama could live without climbing up and down stairs, where she felt comfortable and safe. *A lien-free house!*

It was *possible*. It was *HARD*. But it was *WORTH IT*. In the end, my mother had a house that she truly liked! Before you can live your dreams and go after your goals, you have to see the possibility that you can achieve your dreams.

You must acknowledge, too, that it is going to be hard, that life will throw punches at you. But you must know that the difficulties you encounter will be worth it because in the process of dreaming and striving and fighting for what you want, you will be LIVING your dream and using life up instead of allowing life to use you up. In *The Road Less Traveled*, M. Scott Peck wrote: "Life is difficult. This is a great truth, one of the greatest truths. It is a great truth because once we truly see this truth, we transcend it. Once we truly know that life is difficult—once we truly understand and accept it—then life is no longer difficult. Because once it is accepted, the fact that life is difficult no longer matters."

## Life's Whuppings

When life throws sudden changes at you, don't let it intimidate you. It happens to everybody. We all experience hard knocks, things that deplete your spirit, drain your energy and sap your courage. You just have to dig deep into yourself in those times. At some point you have to admit out loud that life is going to be *hard*. It is going to be *challenging*. And it is going to *work out*. You will work it out. If you don't, life will use you and abuse you.

I remember when I was a child, my Mama used to whup me. When she took after me, I rarely understood. I thought it was horrible that she would beat me. She beat me like she didn't know me. I'd say, "Mama, it's *me*! It's *me*! *Leslie! YOUR OWN BOY!*"

Meanwhile, my mother had her own thing going, "Didn't I tell you not to run with those gang kids? Every time I hear a siren, I think you're in the back of some ambulance with a bullet in you. Didn't I tell you about being down there with the Fourteenth Street Gang?"

But you know, now when I look back I understand why Mama was so panicked and perturbed with me. I know why she was so vehement, and why she gave me such a whupping. She was right about those gang members. Most of them are dead or in jail or on drugs now. Mama was right. She knew who I was; she just didn't like where I was headed. Those were *valuable* whuppings she gave me.

Let me tell you something: You never stop getting whuppings in life. And usually, while you are getting them you don't understand. You think maybe there has been a mistake. They've got the wrong person. You scream, *"Why is this happening to ME?"* You become angry and defiant and resentful, and feel sorry for yourself. And then, later on, you look back and you say, "Now I know why I had to go through that. I needed that lesson. It opened me up to new possibilities. I guess it was worth it after all."

## It's Possible

In challenging times when even our biggest corporations, not to mention entire nations, are in turmoil, it is more important than ever to believe in the possibilities for better times. When chaos prevails in your world or in your personal life, *you must know within yourself that if others can live their dreams, you can live yours too*. Invest your energy in reaching for the greatest possibilities rather than in fretting over your worst fears.

Whatever you have done up to this point in your life is a reflection of what you believe you deserve and what you believe is *possible* for your life. I want you to see yourself with a larger vision. When people of limited vision get laid off from their jobs, they say, "My life is over." Others look for the possibilities.

I knew two men, close friends in Chicago, who were both laid off from their good-paying sales jobs in a highly competitive industry. They identified closely with their jobs, and when they were laid off, they felt cut off from an entire culture. Their self-images and relationships were interwoven with their work.

One of them, however, retained his sense of self even though his job was eliminated. The other identified so closely with his job that when he lost it, he felt he'd lost everything.

In the beginning, after they were fired, both men went out looking for other jobs. And both were rejected again and again. One stopped looking. He stayed home and watched television. He talked on the phone to his negative friends, who reinforced his self-defeating thoughts. The other guy kept looking and kept moving so that negative thoughts could not catch up to him.

One day, the negative-thinking man offered to drive his wife and their children to school. He said he needed the car. His wife took heart in that. She thought maybe he had decided to be positive and look for work again. He dropped his wife off at her office, drove the children to school, and then drove home. He drove into the garage, shut the garage door, stopped up the exhaust pipe of the running car, and took his own life. He was only thirty-seven years old.

The other man kept looking. He finally offered to work for *free*. "I'll volunteer. I don't want to sit home and do nothing." He was the first one to show in his new office, the last one to leave, the best employee—volunteer or paid—they'd ever had. Four weeks later, a regular employee quit and the volunteer got his job.

One man lost his job. The other man lost himself. The difference between these two men was the difference between *eyesight* and *mindsight*. One operated on the basis of what he saw. The other operated on the basis of the possibilities he envisioned. That is what you have to do with your dreams. I want you to do things that give your life meaning and value. *Operate out of your imagination, not your memory.*

You showed up on this planet with greatness within you. The possibilities were endless when you were born, and unless you allow life to batter you into submission, that does not change. You are in control until you abdicate control, and even then you can seize it back.

Have you ever heard someone concede defeat with the comment "I'm only human"? This seems to imply that being human means we come with certain limitations that are insurmountable. I disagree. I believe that most of the limitations we have are self-imposed. Throughout history the human mind and the human spirit have overcome and endured problems and situations that seemed insurmountable. The tools are there, but it takes a focused will, *a consciousness wielded as a dynamic force.*

## The Possibilities of Peanuts

I'm reminded of a man who found a solution to what had been viewed as an insurmountable problem in the South around the turn of the century. The practice of growing cotton year after year after year had depleted the soil of nutrients in much of the South and that, coupled with the devastating effect of the boll-weevil beetle, had reduced the cotton crop to dismal levels.

It appeared the agricultural economy that supported the vast majority of southerners was in dire jeopardy. George

Washington Carver, a scientist and teacher at the Tuskegee Institute, began urging farmers as early as 1906 to "burn off the weevil-infested cotton and plant peanuts."

At first, the tradition-bound farmers disregarded Carver as a nut himself. Peanuts were nothing more than a child's treat, the farmers said. But as cotton production plummeted, the scientist argued that peanuts absorb nitrogen from the air and store it, enabling them to endure long dry spells. Not only are peanuts an easy crop to grow, Carver argued, they are rich in protein and they enrich the soil rather than leeching nutrients from it. Slowly, farmers began to heed his claims, and after several successful crops, Carver was hailed as a genius.

But then, life tossed up another challenge. Everyone planted peanuts. The market became flooded with peanuts. Peanut demand plummeted. Peanuts rotted in the fields. Farmers became discouraged and negative. "We were fools for listening to you," they told Carver.

George Washington Carver was condemned as short-sighted. Rather than give in and retreat, he proved that he was not only a genius, but a man of great character. He rose to the challenge and returned to his laboratory, where he focused on the possibilities of the peanut.

No life is without confrontations and failures. You will hear catcalls and encounter failure in your life. Be aware. Be ready. Absorb the blows, be wiser for them, and persevere because the possibilities are never exhausted. Like George Washington Carver, you must have the strength of character and purpose to find them.

Carver emerged from his laboratory not in defeat but in triumph. His research led to more than one hundred commercial applications for the peanut. Over the years, he expanded that to three hundred. He produced twelve dyes with peanuts. He made milk, margarine, mayonnaise, soap, cooking and rubbing oils, cosmetics, flour, ink, shoe polish, shaving cream, cheese, chili sauce, shampoo, and bleach.

*Three hundred possibilities out of the lowly, unthinking, inanimate peanut!* What must there be locked within *you*, a dynamic, thinking, feeling, creative human being? You *have* to have more possibilities than a peanut!

## Know the Possibilities That Exist for You

I have an entertaining suggestion for you. Whenever you begin to doubt the possibilities of your life, *ponder the peanut!* Have a peanut butter and jelly sandwich. And then laugh at your self-doubts and self-imposed limitations.

I believe you are destined for greatness but there are forces working out there to impede your journey to greatness. It is *hard* to live your dream. But the fact that it is hard does not matter if you expect tough times, face them and take them on.

As George Washington Carver and other visionaries have often discovered, others are not always going to recognize your vision. When Michelangelo selected the stone from which he carved his masterpiece statue of David, it had been sitting unnoticed by the other artists for years. No one else saw the figure in the stone as the sculptor envisioned it. But he knew. He said, "The more the marble wastes, the more the statue grows." He knew that as he chipped the marble away, the statue inside would reveal itself to his artistic vision.

Most people won't share your visions either. They judge by appearance; again, it is a case of *eyesight* versus *mindsight*. Look at your life and your future and say aloud, "It is possible to live my dreams." When you face defeat and disappointment, and the "can't do its" are nagging you, simply consider the unlimited possibilities and say, "It is possible."

It is possible to address your problems and the larger problems in society, and it is possible to solve them if goals are set, if the motivation is strong enough and if we pursue them relentlessly. The homeless, the dropout rate, the teen-age-pregnancy rate, the presence of gangs in our neighbor-hoods and schools, the soaring homicide rate, racial and sexual discrimination; there are ways to deal with and solve these incredible problems. These are all problems caused by people, and people can find ways to solve them just as you can find ways to deal with all of YOUR problems too, if you can see the possibilities.

## Mr. Murphy and His Gang

Several years ago, when I was just starting to progress in my public-speaking career, I learned of a convention in which ten thousand sales representatives gather and some of the best speakers in the country are asked to talk to them. I wanted badly to be a part of it, so I tried for days to reach the people putting it on. I was fired up by the possibilities.

After weeks of trying, I finally made contact with a woman named Evelyn, who was in charge of the affair, and she agreed to let me appear. She said she liked my fire. And then she presented me with an interesting challenge. She told me that at this event, I could undoubtedly sell at least $50,000 worth of my motivational cassette tapes.

"FIFTY-THOUSAND?" I said.

"You'll be able to sell that and more," she assured me.

I called the guy who duplicates my tapes. I told him that I needed thousands of tapes to sell at this meeting.

He said, "Les, you don't have that kind of credit."

I said, "I know, but I can sell them. I'll give you the money right after the engagement."

He didn't believe me. So I got Evelyn on the telephone, along with him. She told him that I should bring that many tapes because I would sell them for certain. She assured me that I was booked. She said she would send the contract in the mail.

I told my tape man, "O ye of little faith."

He agreed to make the tapes.

I ran out to the mailbox the next day, looking for the contract. It wasn't there. *Too soon, Les. Be patient.*

I ran out the day after that. Not there yet. And the next day. No contract. I got nervous. *"Mr. Murphy, you and your Murphy's Law better not be knocking at my door now. Not now, please!"*

Two weeks passed. I finally telephoned Evelyn's office. A secretary answered. I said, "Hello, this is Les Brown. Has Evelyn sent my contract yet?"

There was a pause on the other end of the line. "Oh, Les, haven't you heard? Evelyn died."

"She *died*?"

Another long pause. Though I'd never met Evelyn, I felt that we'd become friends. I felt terrible. And to tell you the truth, I felt a bit abandoned too.

"Did she say anything about my contract before she died?" I asked meekly.

I didn't mean to sound cold and I meant no disrespect for Evelyn, but this was a real shocker for me. Mr. Murphy had laid a good one on me.

"No, the contract was never completed," the secretary said.

I went to Evelyn's funeral and grieved for her. And to be honest, I grieved some too for my lost contract. When I got home I was wiped out. But Mr. Murphy was in the house waiting for me. He mocked me. *"Is it possible you would like to listen to some of your motivational tapes?"*

Of course, I eventually ended my little pity party and once I went back to work and doubled my efforts, I sold all of those tapes and paid off my debts. It was not easy, no. Once you have been knocked out by life, it is hard to pull yourself together and go back again. But you can do it; believe me, you can.

## No Wallowing Allowed

A few years ago, I went through a divorce. I was having a rough time and moping about, unconsciously wallowing in my woe-is-me's, when one of my students saw what I was up to and snapped me out of it. Patricia wrote me a note that read, *"Until you handle it with grace, it will stay in your face."* Instead of growing through a bad experience, instead of learning everything I could from it and moving on, I was mired in my misery. My student told me something I should have known—that you must confront rocky times, establish a mastery over them and then move on.

It is a power that we all have. And it is a power we need to call upon time and again. Stop focusing on the problems and start looking for a solution. When you ask, "Why me?," God's answer might be, "Well, if not you, who would you suggest?"

Victor Frankl was a psychiatrist who was captured by the Nazis and put in a concentration camp. His wife, his parents and a brother were murdered by the Nazis and he was tortured. Yet he survived by deciding that the one thing that his captors could not extinguish was his spirit, his will, the power of his consciousness. It was Frankl who called life's inevitable blows "unavoidable suffering." Everybody has their taste of disappointment and pain and defeat. But, as Frankl said, you still have the power to choose how you will respond, with resignation or defiance.

Author Charles Swindoll, writing on the subject of attitude, says it is

> more important than facts. It is more important than the past, than education, than money, than circumstances, than failures, than successes, than what other people think or say or do. It is more important than appearance, giftedness or skill. It will make or break a company . . . a church . . . a home. The remarkable thing is, you have a choice every day regarding the attitude you will embrace for that

*day. We cannot change our past . . . we cannot change*
*the fact that people will act in a certain way. We cannot*
*change the inevitable. The only thing we can do is play on*
*the one string we have, and that is our attitude. . . . I am*
*convinced that life is 10 percent what happens to me and*
*90 percent how I react to it. And so it is with you. . . .*

If life gets hard, who cares? Go after it. I want to give
you a few tools to overcome the hardships in life. First of all,
it may help you to have a plan in seeking your dreams and
goals. The renowned minister Robert Schuller used to say
*people do not plan to fail, but they do fail to plan.*

Everyone needs some sort of strategy for their lives. Stop
and draw up a blueprint for living your dream. Ask yourself
these questions once a year. Write down your answers, save
them and review them regularly.

- Where have I been so far with my life?
- Why am I here right now?
- Where am I going?
- Has life given me what I am looking for?
- Am I challenging myself?
- Is my life an adventure or is it boring?

Just by reviewing these questions from time to time, you
will heighten your strategic alertness. You need to use your
brain and stretch it out. If I strapped you down in a chair
and kept you there for a long period, I guarantee you would
not be able to walk when I first released you. Your legs would
be wobbly. They would have lost strength from lack of use.
The same holds true for the brain. If you don't give it challenges, it doesn't stay creative and sharp.

Staying sharp is important because life keeps after you.
It doesn't take time off to go fishing. In fact, sometimes life
seems unrelenting. It seems like Mr. Murphy is going door-
to-door in the neighborhood of your heart, hitting everyone
who means something to you.

I received a telephone call one night from a woman friend, thirty years old. The news she had stunned me. She had discovered she was HIV positive. Then, the following night, I received another call; this one knocked me off my feet. A friend of mine had hanged himself.

One friend was fighting for her life, and the other had thrown his away. I know that life is challenging, but you must know that the joys of life are worth the struggle. *The joy of fostering a loving relationship is worth it. The love of a child is worth it. The experience of a wonderful day is worth it. The reward of helping another is worth it.* How can people walk away from these gifts of life? Why do they give up so easily, so soon?

## Patiently Nurture Your Dreams

Maybe we have come to expect too much too soon in our lives. We microwave our meals, speed-dial our telephones, and zap the channels on our television sets. We've become accustomed to instantaneous results. But instant breakfast is one thing; I don't believe we can expect instant gratification and instant fulfillment in our lives. In spite of what they show you on television, there is no quick fix between commercial breaks. You must have patience and engage in persistent action toward making your dream become a reality.

In his book *An Enemy Called Average*, John L. Mason writes of a tree in Asia called the giant bamboo that has a particularly hard seed. It's so hard that to grow that you must water and fertilize that seed every day for four years before any portion of it breaks the soil. And then in the fifth year, the tree shows itself. But the remarkable thing—and consult your *National Geographic* if you don't believe me—is that once it breaks the surface, this bamboo plant, like many of the species, is capable of growing at rates as fast as *four feet a day* to a height of ninety feet in less than a month! *You can practically stand there and watch it grow!*

Now the cosmic question here is, Did the bamboo tree grow ninety feet in under a month? Or did it grow over five years? *Over five years, of course!* Most people do not realize that if the grower had stopped watering or fertilizing that seed at any point, the tree would have died.

When they don't see instant results, many people become discouraged with their dreams and goals. They become impatient. And I believe many of them walk away from their dreams just as they are about to break through and flourish. You must have patience. Your time is going to come if you work diligently and meticulously. It doesn't matter if no one else recognizes that. It matters only that you see it and you have the patience to wait for it.

The author Og Mandino said, "I will persist until I succeed." Continue getting better and NEVER stop looking for ways to win. It doesn't matter if friends or family abandon you, as some of mine deserted me. It hurt very badly, but I kept on pushing. I think giving up would hurt far more than anything that anybody else can do to you. When you operate out of that level of focused consciousness, a new order is established. You become master of your own destiny. Things materialize for you at a much faster rate. To quote Henry David Thoreau:

> *I learned this, that if you advance confidently in the direction of your dreams, and endeavor to live the life which you have imagined, you will meet with a success unexpected in common hours. You will put some things behind, you will pass an invisible boundary, new, universal, and more liberal laws will begin to establish themselves around and within you; or the old laws will be expanded, and interpreted in your favor in a more liberal sense, and you will live with the license of a higher order of beings.*

Your typical negative thinker would never believe that a dream can be nurtured over years and years and then flourish rapidly. But it has happened to me. I struggled for years to establish myself as a public speaker. Even in high school I wanted to participate in the Elks Oratorical Contest, but I never got to. Mr. Washington believed that I had talent, but he did not believe I had the right stuff for THAT particular contest. He didn't see it for me, but I kept after my dream.

It took many years of speaking for free and speaking to small groups and then slightly larger groups. It took years of refining my skills, but suddenly, it has begun to pay off in ways that I never even *dared* dream. I can hardly keep up with all of the opportunities that have opened up for me. Sometimes I have to lock myself in a room or cover myself in a mud bath just to ponder them all.

And, you know, I think if I competed in that Elks Oratorical Contest now, I'd do fairly well. I might even take home a trophy! *Be patient. It will happen for you.* Sooner or later, life will get weary of beating on you and holding the door shut on you, and then it will let you in and throw you a real party!

## It's Done

If you avoid the snares of lethargy, fear, cynicism and negativity, if you strive and build momentum, you cannot be stopped. A pebble may derail a train just as it begins to move, but once that engine gets up a full head of steam it will drive through all sorts of barriers. With momentum driving you toward your goal, it's done. The course of history is set.

Have you ever seen a basketball player take a long shot in a game and then turn and run downcourt to play defense without watching to see whether the ball goes in? How can a player do that? Because he is absolutely certain that *it's done.* Count it.

When you are so focused that you no longer concern yourself with the obstacles, you simply overcome them and go on. When you no longer care whether anyone approves, then you have hit the wall and gone beyond. Your journey to your dream is done, *fait accompli.*

You will reach a point in your journey when your consciousness takes on its own energy. I have an artist friend who describes to me these transcendent moments in her painting when the brush seems to operate of its own volition. My writer friends say they experience similar moments when the words flow from an unknown source that seems beyond their conscious selves. The gift flows, the talent speaks, the muse works her own magic. You become the instrument of a greater power.

## *GeorgeArt*

George Colin dreamed of painting. Some said it was a strange dream for a flour bagger in a Pillsbury plant, but that is what George Colin dreamed, and that is what he did— in his spare time, on his days off, before he went to work, after work. Unable to afford real canvas and expensive brushes and art supplies, he often painted on paper he found in Dumpsters behind a printing plant. He painted with children's watercolors, marker pens, house paint, spray paint, anything that translated his dream.

For ten, twenty, thirty years, George Colin painted and painted in an old leaky house next to the converted garage where he lived with his wife, Winnie. George was proud of what he painted, so he gave his paintings to relatives and friends as gifts. Some were grateful, but others mocked him.

One relative hung George's gift painting in his hog lot, and his hogs ate it. George also hung his paintings on trees in his yard, and sold them along the highway that runs through the small town where he lives in central Illinois.

On weekends, a lot of people drove through his town, Salisbury, on their way to a state park. Some bought George's paintings for fifty cents or a dollar. He was glad to get that kind of money, but he was happier that people wanted his artwork.

George sold his paintings at curbside for years, and eventually people began driving to Salisbury just to see him and his work. Professors from nearby colleges, and folk-art lovers from Chicago, nearly two hundred miles away, began to collect his paintings. They often bought dozens at a time. Word spread of George's dream paintings. Soon, art-gallery dealers began appearing at his door, offering to display his work in their galleries in St. Louis and Chicago. George was glad they came, though he was sometimes baffled by all the fuss.

On Wells Street in the trendy Old Town neighborhood of Chicago, near the famous Second City comedy theater, Italian restaurants, book stores and shops, there is now an art gallery called "GeorgeArt." This gallery is devoted solely to the works of George Colin. His paintings sell for hundreds and even thousands of dollars.

George is retired from the Pillsbury plant where he worked for decades. A humble, unassuming man, he still lives in the converted garage by the highway in Salisbury, and he still paints every day. He is delighted that people like what he does, but he would probably be doing it even if they didn't. He lives his dream as he has always lived it—happily.

I believe that, as Henry David Thoreau has said, if you live and pursue your dreams, the universe will line up on your side. The universe will yield to you. You will live with the license of a higher order of being. Things will happen for you, just as they happened for George Colin, an unstoppable man who knew that the most important factor in reaching his dream was himself.

## It's You

When you are absolutely convinced of the possibility and necessity of pursuing your dream, you take on a different kind of driving energy. You add years to your life, but more important, you add purpose and meaning to it.

How do you make this dream come true? What necessary actions should be taken? The determining factor is you. You will make the difference. You will make it happen. No one else is going to take care of your business. It would be great if our relatives and friends would all support us, or co-sign for us, or loan us some money. It would be great if people said, "Is that your dream? C'mon, let's go get it." But it isn't that kind of party. You must take on the responsibility for making your dream reality. The major factor in helping you achieve your dreams is YOU.

Be an innovator. Be creative. Take your particular talents and interests to a level where they have never been taken before. Feel that you are THE ONE. I believe in the leap-frog theory in which you leap out ahead of the pack and say, "I'm THE ONE."

Benjamin Weir was held captive in Lebanon for sixteen months. The first twelve months he was chained to a radiator by his wrists and his ankles. He was shackled wearing only his undershorts. When he was released, finally, he said that he overcame his despair by looking down every link in the chain and envisioning each individual link as another bead in his rosary. He said that he looked at each link and identified something in his life that he was thankful for.

In the midst of torture and confinement, Weir had every

reason to despair, but instead, he counted his blessings and focused on the positive. Asked at a press conference what he might say now to his captors, Weir replied, "I would say good-bye." He wasted no anger. He offered no more hatred to the world.

There are people who have seemed defeated time and time again. They have had doors slammed in their faces. They have lost all their money. What enables these people to face danger and criticism and ridicule and keep on keeping on? What makes them capable of facing, what Hamlet calls "the slings and arrows of outrageous fortune"?

We are not a race of pain seekers. What is it about these people that enables them to endure that kind of punishment, and even thrive in the face of it? Ask them, and they will tell you, *"It's worth it."*

If you interviewed Nelson Mandela and asked what empowered him to endure prison for twenty-six years rather than accept the conditions that would have won him release to his family and escape from the threat of death, he would tell you that he was nurtured by the knowledge that his was a just and worthy cause. The knowledge that *it was worth it* got him through it. People who quit before realizing their goals often say that they simply decided, "It wasn't worth it." If it isn't worth it, then it isn't really YOUR dream. Your true dream is *always* worth it. It is your destiny.

It is worth it to pursue your dreams because that is how you grow in life. Many people fight for their goals and dreams with so much determination that they awe me. Among all of the cheerless glitter of Atlantic City there is a lady whose misfortunes are exceeded only by the strength of her determination. She has no arms and no legs, and she works on the city's famed Boardwalk each day. She works for tips, playing the piano by using her tongue. In this manner, she has provided for her two children.

To people of a certain frame of mind, perhaps those who prefer the facade of Atlantic City's casinos to the reality of the town's deep poverty, this lady is considered an eyesore.

Others cheer her courage. She has vowed never to go on public aid, to always support her family however she can.

When an effort was made by some in city government to prevent this woman from working on the Boardwalk, she fought them and won. To her, it was well worth it.

## Focus on Goals, Not Hardship

Another friend of mine, Mildred Singleton, refused to let her dreams die even though she was faced with tremendous personal turmoil. Instead of her anguish, she focused on what gave her and her two daughters the most joy in life as she framed and homed in on her goals.

Mildred was in medical school en route to her goals when her husband died. In fact, he died just as she was about to take her medical-board exams, one of the final steps to becoming a doctor. I was inspired by her ability to persevere through the pain of the loss of a loved one.

She did it by focusing on what would bring joy to her life, *the possibilities* that she had envisioned for her life. As a high-school student on a field trip, Mildred had observed surgeons at work to restore a patient's vision. She felt it was her destiny to do that sort of work. She thought it would bring her great joy to help people regain their vision.

She was one of eight children. Her mother died when she was in her teens. Her father had believed strongly in her ability. He told her that if she made all As someone would notice her and give her a scholarship. She did exactly that and received a full scholarship. Mildred passed that medical exam on her first attempt because she had become the sort of person who believed she deserved to achieve her goal in spite of adversity and pain. She held no pity parties. She remained in control of her life. She wept and she grieved over the death of her husband, but she kept her focus and she achieved her goal. She was passionate, she was determined and she discovered *it was worth it*.

The responsibility for reaching our dreams lies with the individuals who dreamed the dream. Yours lies with you. Do not let it be buried with you. I believe a lot of people don't muster the courage to live their dreams because they are afraid to die.

Jack Boland, the founder of the Church of Today in Warren, Michigan, was one of my great sources of inspiration and support. He died of cancer a short time ago, but before he died he invited his congregation, family and friends together for what some termed his "living funeral."

It may sound morbid to those who didn't know Jack, but it was actually an incredibly touching and inspiring event. Everyone there knew that Jack had been fighting for his life, but few knew that the doctors had determined that Jack had only a few weeks to live.

At the gathering, Jack had his doctor tell us the grim diagnosis. And Jack's response was, *"What is, is. I accept that, but I have the choice to fight the odds and not surrender."*

Jack did not surrender, of course. Instead, he told us that he planned to keep on enjoying life down to the final second. Jack was not afraid of death because he had not been afraid of life.

He lived life so fully and so joyfully that he said he actually *enjoyed* his cancer treatments. He was determined to enjoy them, and he did, he said, because even though they were torturous, they were part of living, a part of the continuous struggle of life.

"I enjoyed the days of chemotherapy," he said. "I think I am the only living being who has ever gone into chemotherapy with the commitment to enjoy it and I did, I *flat* did. I learned to enjoy all difficulties."

In his emotional address that day, Jack reminded us that our lives are God's gift to us but what we do with our lives is our gift to God.

"It often amazes me that so many of us have not yet

learned to live our lives," Jack said. "We tend to let our lives happen to us from the outside, drifting and wandering and often times complaining and cursing our lot, when if we but knew it, our lot would be startlingly wonderful."

Jack said that we are given this gift of life, but so often we don't actively live it and enjoy it. It is like being given a wonderful grand piano and never learning to play it, or a fine car and never driving it.

Knowing that his own time was coming to an end, Jack challenged us that day to take great advantage of the time that we had left. The theme he gave to the day was "If Not Now, When?" He asked repeatedly, "If not now, when will you begin living your life?" And he challenged us to also live beyond our own selfish interests. "If you have never been part of something that you would give your life for, then I think it would be difficult for you to find and discover the quality of life you are looking for," he said. "We have to live beyond ourselves, reach beyond ourselves and attach ourselves to our star."

And he challenged us to enjoy life as much as he did; down to the last seconds. "Whatever state you find yourself in, *enjoy your way out of it*," he said. "The perfect solution to a wonderful life is to experience joy. . . . I'm going to enjoy the last day down to the last minute and last second. I'm going to enjoy dying. What an interesting experience that is going to be."

A few weeks after that gathering, Jack's health declined rapidly and he was hospitalized. His family gathered around his bed, certain that the end was near for him. At one point he regained consciousness and thanked them for being a good family. He told them not to feel sorry for him. "I'm looking forward to the great adventure," he said.

He closed his eyes, then opened them a short while later, looked at those gathered around, and made them smile one more time: "This is embarrassing! I'm not dead yet!"

We believe Jack left his family and friends one final message. It was expected that he would die in the final weeks of

February, but he fought harder and much more successfully than his doctors had expected.

Jack made his final statement when he died on March 4. And therein, I believe, is his final message to those who were touched by this man's great spirit.

I believe he wants us to *march forth*. Face the challenges life presents you. Relish every minute of life. Take life on. *MARCH FORTH*. LIVE YOUR DREAMS!

[See exercises for this chapter in the Action Planner on page 268.]

# LIVE YOUR DREAMS ACTION PLANNER

To inquire about PBS specials, the tape version of *Live Your Dreams*, or other seminars, programs, video and audio tapes offered by Les Brown Unlimited Inc., call 800-733-4226 or write Les Brown Unlimited, 2180 Penobscot Building, Detroit, MI 48226.

For videocassettes and audiocassettes of Les Brown's PBS television specials, call 800-327-5110, or write TeleVideo, Ltd., 411 South Sangamon Street, Chicago, IL 60607.

# Chapter 1: Mrs. Mamie Brown's Baby Boy

═══════════════

## Drop Your Burdens

Just as I got tag-teamed by those neighbor boys because I would not put down my Mama's groceries, many of us carry around emotional baggage that prevents us from pursuing our dreams. Reflect on your own life and think about the baggage that you need to unload so that you can grow.

Write down those things that are holding you back, and then reflect on how you should get rid of them.

_____

_____

_____

_____

_____

_____

Keep this list handy to remind yourself that you have dropped these burdens and you are now free to fight for what you deserve in life: the best that your greatness can bring you!

## Who Do You Want to Be?

Now that you have dropped your burdens, you must decide what it is you want. But first, you must understand that you only get what you ARE. You have to be confident that you deserve something before you can truly dedicate yourself to getting it. So, what type of PERSON do you want to become? How do you want to change? On the lines below, describe the NEW YOU, and keep the description handy so that you can check it every day to see how much closer you are getting to your dreams.

_____

_____

_____

_____

_____

_____

## Goal Gauge

To get a feeling for what it is that you REALLY want in life, go through the following list and rate each item as a number one, two or three goal with one being top priority in your life.

Find a job I enjoy        _____

Strengthen my relationships    _____

Find financial security      _____

Become more physically fit     \_\_\_\_
Quit smoking or drinking     \_\_\_\_
Enjoy more leisure time     \_\_\_\_
Get closer to my children     \_\_\_\_
Get more education     \_\_\_\_
Buy a nicer house     \_\_\_\_
Move to a better place     \_\_\_\_
Live a more meaningful life     \_\_\_\_
Make more friends     \_\_\_\_
Lead a more adventurous life     \_\_\_\_
Feel better about myself     \_\_\_\_
Find true love     \_\_\_\_
Become more spiritual     \_\_\_\_
Do more for others     \_\_\_\_
Have a greater impact     \_\_\_\_
Inspire others     \_\_\_\_
Learn new skills     \_\_\_\_

Now number them one through three in importance and concentrate only on the number *ones*.

# Chapter 2: You Gotta Be Hungry!

## Mastering Your Hunger and Yourself

Now that you are developing your HUNGER for your dreams, it is a good idea to be clear about the tools you are going to work with. You can't win a big race with a broken-down jalopy. Take a look at who you are.

List your talents and abilities first. Write down everything that comes to mind and make sure you come up with at least 10 assets. Don't be embarrassed. Be proud. And be aware of your gifts and talents because these are the assets of YOU, Inc.

### Things I'm Good At

1. _____

2. _____

3. _____

4. _____

5. _____

6. _____

7. _____

8. _____

9. _____

10. _____

Now, take a look at the debits of YOU, Inc. What are the things you need to improve on? Are you frequently late for meetings or work? Are you disorganized? Do you tend to make excuses rather than accept responsibility? Do you spend too much time talking and not enough time DOING?

List at least ten of these debits and then vow to work on improving each area. Start with the first one and work on it today. And then go down the list. Check yourself each week to see if you are improving. Working to improve yourself fires up your HUNGER!

*Things I Need to Improve*

1. _____

2. _____

3. _____

4. _____

5. _____

6. _____

7. _____

8. _____

9. _____

10. _____

## Talk to People . . . Talk to More People

Things happen when you talk to people about your dreams and goals. Opportunities unfold. The universe opens up to you. You form a more concrete concept of what you want by verbalizing your dream and you become more eloquent in describing it. And if you talk enthusiastically about what you want to do with your life you create a positive cycle of empowerment. Your enthusiasm will feed your drive and your drive will propel you toward your dream.

So get talking. Start a list below of the first people you need to contact in order to pursue your goals and dreams—professionals in the field, teachers, etc.

_____

_____

_____

_____

_____

_____

_____

_____

_____

_____

# Chapter 3: The Power
# to Change

## Building a New You

If you are going to *have* more than you have now, you've got to *be* more than you are now. What do you have to do to become the person you want to be? What will you have to know? One of the reasons you feel stuck now is because you know there is more to you than you have been showing the world.

Describe the type of person you want to become:

_____

_____

_____

What kind of preparation do you need to do to become that ideal self?

_____

_____

_____

What are your strengths?

_____

_____

_____


What do you love to do? What makes you HAPPY?

_____

_____

_____


How could you make money or spend more time doing what makes you happy?

_____

_____

_____


What can you do *today* to take yourself a little closer to doing what you want to do?

_____

_____

_____

## What to Do When You Are Stuck

1. Evaluate where you are. Ask yourself what brought you to this point. Are you learning or are you merely doing the same thing over and over again? You can't do the same thing over and over and expect that the results will be different. That's CRAZY! What you have done in the past will only get you what you've gotten so far. Change your approach.

2. Accept responsibility for your life. Know that it is YOU who will get you where you want to go, no one else. Say to yourself, *"I got myself into this, I can get myself out of it. I am not going to be a volunteer victim."*

3. Be determined to handle any challenge in a way that will make you grow.

4. If you have a plan, put it to work now. Do whatever works best for you.

5. Take action. Do something that will move you toward handling the challenge today.

6. Help somebody else. If you are spending a lot of energy feeling sorry for yourself, find someone you can help and forget about yourself for a while. What you give is what you get.

7. Take charge of your emotions. Master them or they will master you.

8. Expect things to get better.

9. Reinterpret the past so that things that have been a burden actually empower you.

## Getting Up the Courage

Think about the positive things you could do if you only had the courage to do them. You must take responsibility for your own life if you are going to change. You cannot continue to run on automatic, waiting for life to act on you. You must act on life.

What would you really like to do to earn a living? What relationships would you like to establish? Put your imagination to work in response to the following exercise.

If I had the courage, I
would:                              But this is what stops me:

1. _____        _____

_____        _____

2. _____        _____

_____        _____

3. _____        _____

_____        _____

4. _____        _____

_____        _____

5. _____        _____

_____        _____

Review your answers and then work on developing the courage to overcome the things that are stopping you from taking responsibility for your life and living your dreams. Ask yourself what the worst thing is that could happen if you overcame your fears and went ahead to pursue your dreams. Visualize yourself taking action and going after what you want. Notice how positive you feel about yourself when you visualize yourself going after your dreams? So, DO IT NOW!

# Chapter 4: Wake Up and Work on Your Dreams

## A Checkup List

**\*Check your attitude toward yourself.**

Do you feel good about yourself? Confident? Do you think you are deserving of your dreams? Or do you really, deep down inside, feel as though you do not deserve the best that life has to offer?

My mental attitude toward myself is:

_____

_____

_____

_____

**\*Check your attitude toward life.**

You get what you expect out of life. Do you see life as drudgery or as an adventure?

My mental attitude toward life is:

_____

_____

_____

**\*Check your attitude regarding your physical appearance.**

Are you proud of or ashamed of your physical appearance? What are you telling people by the way you present yourself?

My physical appearance reflects:

_____

_____

_____


**\*Check your attitude regarding your health.**

Do you take care of your body? What do you put into it? Do you eat wholesome, low-fat foods? Do you have a regular exercise program?

This is what I do to take care of my health:

_____

_____

_____


**\*Check your home and work environments.**

Are they well-organized and neatly arranged or are they a mess? Are you satisfied with the way they look? Are they desirable places to be?

Describe how you feel about your daily living and working environments.

_____

_____

_____

**\*Check your career status.**

Are you happy with your job? Are you stimulated and working actively toward career development or are you just putting in your time? If you were the boss, would you consider yourself a valuable employee?

Evaluate your status.

_____

_____

_____

**\*Check your relationships.**

Review each of your relationships. Are they nourishing or toxic? Do they drain you or build you up? Do the people in your life encourage you to go after your dreams or do they hold you back with discouraging words?

List those closest to you and evaluate the relationship you have with each of them.

_____

_____

_____

**\*Check your use of your time.**

Do you go on autopilot when you go home at night? Do you spend the evening watching television? Do you watch things that don't even interest you? How often do you read a book that inspires you?

Write down your nightly routine and study how you might improve it to make it more profitable for your development in your career or personal life.

_____

_____

_____

## Tear Up and Throw Away Those Burdens!

Write down all your bad habits and faults and all the mistakes you have made in your life. Did you hurt someone? Did you malign someone? Did you waste an opportunity? Write all your burdens down.

_____

_____

_____

_____

_____

Did you write down everything that has nagged and eaten at you over the years? Good. Now mentally take this page out of the book, tear it to shreds and throw it away. Forgive yourself for your faults and your mistakes and move on. The way to your dreams is now clear!

## Discover the Winner in You

Sit back and relax. Let your mind float back to a time when you felt great about yourself. It should be a time when you felt competent, successful and secure. Relive a moment when you were at the top of your game. Describe below what you were doing when you felt so good about yourself.

_____

_____

_____

_____

Use this positive memory to offset feelings of inadequacy or depression. Whenever you feel low or insecure, call it to mind. Let it make you feel good about yourself again. Recharge your enthusiasm and believe in yourself. Believe in the greatness within you.

# Chapter 5: Live Your Dreams

## General Goals

**\*Define your goals.**
　　Write down the things that you really want to attain, acquire, achieve or accomplish. What do you want out of life?

_____

_____

_____

## Career Goals

**\*What type of career do you want?**

_____

_____

_____

\*What type of business would you like to be in?

_____

_____

_____


\*What level would you like to reach?

_____

_____

_____


\*Describe your dream job.

_____

_____

_____


\*How much are you willing to invest to get that job?

_____

_____

_____


\*How much money would you like to earn each week, each month or each year?

_____

_____

_____

## *Relationship Goals*

**\*What types of people are you drawn to?**

_____

_____

_____

**\*What types of people do you think you need to attract?**

_____

_____

_____

**\*What do you need to change about yourself to attract the types of people you want in your life?**

_____

_____

_____

Once you have written down your goals, study them and make sure they are what you truly want for your life. Then, start to focus on how to begin working toward your goals. Read your list of goals three times a day. Opportunities will arise!

# A Plan of Action

It is up to you to determine where you want to go and how you are going to get there in your life. You have to assume that responsibility. List at least three goals for each of the following periods. Ask yourself where you want to be and what you want to be doing in each period. *Remember, a goal that is not written down is merely a wish.*

### Short-term Goals (1 month)

1. _____
2. _____
3. _____

### Mid-term Goals (6 to 12 months)

1. _____
2. _____
3. _____

### Long-term Goals (5 to 10 years)

1. _____
2. _____
3. _____

# Chapter 6: Fix Your Focus

## Act on Your Ideas

Unless you focus on your goals and act on them, there can be no growth or change in your life. Focus on your dreams and go after them. Build a new you. Practice these ten methods of focusing on your dreams and goals.

1. See yourself beyond your present circumstances. Visualize what you want.

2. Turn down the negative self-talk and turn up the volume on the positive talk: "I'm doing GREAT!" Tell yourself that several times a day.

3. Increase your sense that you DESERVE your dream.

4. Invest in a personal development library with books that will motivate you, particularly biographies of those who have endured hardship, persevered and then lived their dreams (Helen Keller, Henry Ford, Gandhi, Martin Luther King, Jr., to name a few).

5. Assess yourself. Get to know your strong points and the things you should work on.

6. Demand more from yourself. Don't hold back. You've got plenty of energy. Use it before you lose it.

7. Take risks.

8. Stand up for what you want; don't let anyone turn you around from your pursuit of your dream.

9. Surround yourself with supportive, quality people.

10. Commit yourself to being unstoppable!

REMEMBER THIS: *You can always have more and do more, because you can always BE more!!*

## Do It Now!

List five things you have been meaning to do but have put off. Do them NOW!

1. _____

2. _____

3. _____

4. _____

5. _____

## Claiming Your Dream

Are you not certain that you have a dream? Well, I am certain you have one. You may have lost touch with it, but it is there, believe me. It is important to have dreams and goals because they empower you to seek your greatness in life. Write down five reasons you deserve to accomplish your dream or goal.

Example: I've put up with enough hard times, I've earned the right to expect more!

1. _____

2. _____

3. _____

4. _____

5. _____

Review these reasons every day and build up your determination and the feeling that you deserve your dreams.

## Great Expectations Lead
## to Great Achievements

What do you expect out of your life? Are you known as someone who has never lived up to your innate talents and abilities? If you are going to develop to your full potential you have to see it for yourself. You have to have great expectations for your own life. Write down answers to the following questions and review your attitude toward your life and your future.

- What do you expect to achieve in your life?

_____

_____

_____

_____

- How much money do you expect to have?

_____

_____

_____

_____

- How much career or family success do you expect to have?

_____

_____

_____

_____

• How much happiness do you expect to attain?

_____

_____

_____

_____

• How much love?

_____

_____

_____

_____

• How many friends?

_____

_____

_____

_____

• **Which of these expectations would you like to raise?**

_____

_____

_____

_____

# Chapter 7: Fear of Frogs

## Overcoming Fear of Failure

It is no fun to fail, but you must pick yourself up and get back in the race. The only way you can grow is to challenge yourself beyond your present circumstances. You have to dare to risk failure.

*Write two examples of something you have failed at.

1. _____

2. _____

*Explain in detail how you felt after failing and the results of the failure.

_____

_____

_____

_____

_____

_____

*So, you felt badly. How long did you feel that way? Was it terminal or did you get over it? If you haven't gotten over it yet, you will. You MUST! Write down five things that you are going to do to get on with your life.

1. _____

2. _____

3. _____

4. _____

5. _____


## Overcoming Your Fear of Losing Approval

One of the greatest deterrents to taking action is the fear of losing the approval of our family or friends. Are you truly willing to give up YOUR dreams because of what others might think? Of course not. As you grow you will come into contact with people who will share your expanded level of consciousness, so don't worry. Go after your dreams.

*Write down two things you didn't do or try to do because you were afraid of disapproval. Decide to face your fears and do them NOW!

1. _____

2. _____

# Chapter 8: The Young and the Goal-less

## Know Your Gifts and Share Them

We all have greatness within us. We all arrive with gifts and talents and abilities that are part of our unique packages. Sometimes, however, we fail to recognize and develop those gifts in ourselves because of insecurities, fears, laziness or burdens that block us. People who do not know the value of their gifts are easy prey for life's surprise blows and for predators. Know your gifts, and once you know them, share them so that others may benefit from your example and discover their own greatness.

*List the talents, abilities, and gifts that make you unique. Write down at least five, more if you can. THIS IS NO TIME FOR MODESTY! Besides, no one is watching.

(Examples: I am mechanically inclined. I am good with my hands. I absorb information well. I focus well on assigned tasks. I have leadership abilities.)

1. _____

2. _____

3. _____

4. _____

5. _____

*See! You do have greatness within you! Now, list five ways in which you can apply the above five items to a career or whatever your life's mission might be.

1. _____

2. _____

3. _____

4. _____

5. _____

*Now you know there is a future awaiting you and your greatness. In this step, write down five ways in which you can apply your gifts and experiece to help someone else realize their greatness.

1. _____

2. _____

3. _____

4. _____

5. _____

## Young People's Check Station

Check your relationships. Are the people you associate with pushing you up or dragging you down? List your five best friends or those closest to you. Then write down what you get out of your relationship with each of them. Is it a positive or negative relationship? Does it make you a better person? Are you proud of the things you have done together? Do you smile when you think of them? Or do you feel worse about yourself after you have been with that person?

Check the list when you are done and make a promise to end those relationships that drag you down. You have greatness to pursue. Don't let anyone slow you down. In the end, YOU are responsible for YOUR life. If your talents are wasted, YOU suffer the most and you have only yourself to blame. If your talents are realized and your potential fulfilled, YOU get the rewards and you can take pride in your accomplishments.

List the five people closest to you and the nature of your relationship.

1. _____ + or −

2. _____ + or −

3. _____ + or −

4. _____ + or −

5. _____ + or −

## Get a Plan

You don't need to determine right now what the course of your life will be, but it helps to have some general idea. List a few things you can do that will carry you toward your goals either for a career or for your personal life.

In the next week _____

_____

**In the next month** _____

_____

**In the next year** _____

_____


## *Recognize Your Own Value*

Think of yourself as YOU, Inc. What are your assets? What
are your liabilities? What can you do to build on your
assets and reduce your liabilities?

List your assets and what you can do to maximize them.

_____

_____

_____


List your liabilities and what you can do to minimize
them.

_____

_____

_____

## Seek Advisers, Mentors and Role Models

We all need guides on our journey through life. List five people you believe can help you on your journey to greatness. Give a reason why you think each of them can be of assistance. Try to make contact with each of them within the next few months. Establish relationships that make you better.

1. _____

2. _____

3. _____

4. _____

5. _____

## Adult Check Station

The first thing adults should do when they find themselves in conflict with their children or other young people in their lives is check themselves to see if they are sending out conflicting messages that the young people are merely responding to or reflecting.

Do you always practice what you preach? List five areas in which you need to check yourself.

(Example: I speed when I drive, and then caution my children to obey the speed limits when they drive.)

1. _____

2. _____

3. _____

4. _____

5. _____

## *Get Involved!*

I believe adults and parents who do not get involved in children's lives effectively forfeit any right to attempt to influence their lives. If you don't care enough to get involved, why should young people listen to you?

List five ways in which you can get more involved in the lives of young people in your life or community.

1. _____

2. _____

3. _____

4. _____

5. _____

## Celebrate Their Greatness

Rather than treating the young people in your life as un-formed adults, try celebrating their greatness with them. Let them know that you see something unique and special in them. Help them see the greatness within them.

Name the young people in your life and then list the special gifts and abilities of each of them. Think about how you can help them see themselves as unique individuals worthy of the best that life has to offer.

# Chapter 9: Be Positively Charged!

## Positive Sources of Support, Information and Inspiration

1. People. Look for positive role models. Tell them what you admire about them and ask them for guidance. Don't be shy. They will be flattered.

Write down the names of some who can help you find your way to a greater vision of yourself.

_____

_____

_____

2. Organizations. Business and professional organizations exist to encourage networking and information exchange. You can tap into this positive source and move way ahead on the learning curve. Ask people in your field for the names of clubs you can join. Write them down.

_____

_____

_____

3. Books. Your neighborhood library is still the best and the cheapest positive source of information available. Read and learn! If you read one book a week in your field of interest, you've moved way ahead of those who haven't. List books that can help you.

_____

_____

_____

_____

_____

_____

_____

# Chapter 10: It's Possible!

## Life's Whuppings

Each of us experiences defeats in life. We can transform defeat into victory if we learn from life's whuppings. List five defeats you have experienced and next list what you learned from each of them.

My defeats:

1. _____

2. _____

3. _____

4. _____

5. _____


My lessons learned:

1. _____

2. _____

3. _____

4. _____

5. _____

## Mindsight Versus Eyesight

You must learn to live for what you can imagine, rather than being held back by what you see and know right now. Practice seeing yourself with mindsight rather than eyesight by doing this exercise.

For each eyesight example given, list a mindsight alternative.

### Eyesight

Example: I have only a high school diploma.
1. I am only a secretary.
2. I don't work well with other people.
3. I am not good at sales.
4. I have poor mathematical skills.
5. I don't have enough money for college.

### Mindsight

Example: I can go to junior college or trade school at night.

1. _____

2. _____

3. _____

4. _____

5. _____

## Know Your Possibilities

Based on your unique talents and gifts and abilities, list TEN possibilities for your life.

1. _____

2. _____

3. _____

4. _____

5. _____

6. _____

7. _____

8. _____

9. _____

10. _____


## Dream a Little Dream, Live a Big Life

Allow yourself to dream by completing these sentences.

If I had my life to live over, I would _____

_____.

If I had my wish, I would _____

_____.

My life would be more fulfilling if _____

_____.

One person I highly respect is _____

_____.

I spend most of my time _____

_____.

One goal I really want is _____

_____.

I am happiest when _____

_____.

One area I need to improve in my life is _____

_____.

I am most proud of my ability to _____

_____.

Three things I would like said about me if I died to-day are:

1. _____

2. _____

3. _____

Read this exercise over and get to know yourself better so that you know exactly who you are and what you want. Then GO AFTER YOUR DREAMS!